Democratic Education
in Schools and Classrooms

In their daily experiences in school and out, students are gaining lasting impressions of how democratic values are actually interpreted.

NATIONAL COUNCIL FOR THE SOCIAL STUDIES
BULLETIN NO. 70

Democratic Education in Schools and Classrooms

MARY A. HEPBURN
EDITOR

NATIONAL COUNCIL FOR THE SOCIAL STUDIES

Library of Congress Catalog Card Number 83-062201
ISBN 0-87986-046-4
Copyright © 1983 by the
NATIONAL COUNCIL FOR THE SOCIAL STUDIES
3501 Newark Street, NW, Washington, DC 20016

Contents

About the Authors

Mary A. Hepburn is Professor of Social Science Education and researcher in the Citizen Education Program, Institute of Government, University of Georgia. She has been active in the College and University Faculty Assembly of NCSS, serving on the Executive Board from 1978–81. She has published numerous research articles on political/citizenship education and two textbooks on local government. Currently she is serving on the NCSS Citizenship Committee, the Board of Directors of the Social Science Education Consortium, and the Education Task Force of Project '87 of the American Political Science Association and American Historical Association.

Douglas H. Jenisch teaches regional history, government, and global studies at Hanover H.S., Hanover, New Hampshire. He also runs a Volunteer Service Program at Hanover High.

Zada Koblas, who taught social studies in the Minneapolis school system for 20 years, has recently retired. She has been active in NCSS and the Minnesota Council for many years. She was President of the Minnesota Council from 1976–1978. In NCSS she was on the Task Force on Accountability and served several terms in the House of Delegates. She received the NCSS Outstanding Service Award in 1979 at the national meeting in Portland.

Ellen Grundfest Sampson is Assistant to the Minnesota Commissioner of Employee Relations in Minneapolis. She conducted the school case study described in this Bulletin while she was a graduate researcher at Indiana University's Social Studies Development Center.

Michael A. Radz is Assistant Superintendent for Instruction, Olympia Community Unit School District, Stanford, Illinois. He has served as a member of the NCSS Citizenship Education Committee and the Committee on Rural Social Studies Education. The Illinois State Board of Education presented him with the Those Who Excel award for his contributions to the development of the state's Responsibility Education program.

Ronald L. VanSickle is Associate Professor of Social Science Education and Co-Director of the Center for Economic Education, University of Georgia. He is a former high school social studies teacher and social studies consultant. He conducts research in the areas of teaching methods, curriculum courses, the social psychology of classroom instruction and reflective thinking. VanSickle also develops instructional materials in economic education. He is currently Research Editor of *Social Education.*

Foreword

To prepare students to be humane, rational citizens in a global context—that is our mission as social studies educators. To assist us in that work, the National Council for the Social Studies has published numerous articles, bulletins, and yearbooks on how best to convey knowledge and develop abilities needed by citizens. Much has been written about the need to give students practice in reflective inquiry, value analysis, and decision-making if we want citizens to be able to solve complex problems in a democratic context. This Bulletin goes one step further by affirming that in order for youth to develop a commitment to democracy, they must experience it in their schools; as citizenship educators, we have a particular responsibility to work for greater democratization of classrooms and schools.

The publication of this Bulletin is timely.

First, it comes to us at a time when we see democracy being threatened by both political alienation and self-righteous authoritarianism. This is a time when we need to reassert to administrators, school boards, and parents—as well as to ourselves—that the maintenance of a democratic way of life is dependent on instilling democratic values in children and youth. Because those values are acquired through experience, students must daily observe democratic practices and adult models who adhere to the values of justice, equity, freedom, responsibility, and participation. Social studies educators should take the lead in showing others how to create schools that teach democracy through demonstration.

Second, this Bulletin is timely because it comes to us when the diverse activities of NCSS are focusing on Academic Freedom: The Freedom to Teach and The Freedom to Learn. These freedoms enable classes to explore controversial issues in an open, supportive environment. The implication from research for practice is clear: the experience of participating in controversial issues discussions is crucial to the development of democratic attitudes in secondary students. Teachers, administrators, authors, publishers, parents, and other community members must each do their part to ensure that youth experience the freedom to inquire. As explained in Alan Griffin's classic dissertation justifying reflective inquiry in the schools, "societies are democratic in terms of only one test—the degree to which they refrain from setting limits upon the matters that may be thought about" (1942). Our schools must reflect that commitment to democracy.

Third, the publication of this Bulletin is timely because of the forthcoming bicentennials of the framing of the United States Constitution, its adoption, and the adoption of the Bill of Rights. If we begin to work now to move our classes and our schools a little further along the continuum of democratic practices, then in 1987, 1989, and 1991, the young will join us in a true celebration of constitutional principles. On the other hand, if we do not make those changes, we risk that once more youth will witness hypocrisy, mock our rhetoric, and become further alienated. Clearly, the time for action is now.

While it is appropriate to tie this issue to the forthcoming American celebrations, we recognize that the democratization of schools is not a uniquely American concern, anymore than is the democratization of society. We have now worked to overcome the latter myth through lessons on international human rights, and as a result, our students are learning that citizens of many nations are politically socialized to the values of justice, equality before the law, due process, freedom of thought and religion,

Participation in school extra-curricular activities contributes to the development of democratic political attitudes.

freedom of opinion and expression, freedom of peaceful assembly, and the freedom to participate in their government. Now is the time for us as global educators to learn more about the activities of our international colleagues in the process of democratic socialization. The research and examples used in this Bulletin are primarily drawn from experiences in the United States. As a next step we need international readers to share with us similar research and case studies from schools and classes in other nations.

This Bulletin sets forth the philosophic grounds for democratizing schools and the evidence from research as to why we should undertake the task. Various chapters describe how individual teachers can restructure their classes and ways in which entire schools have been successful in increasing student participation in decision-making. The chapter on the important role of the principal in this process should be shared with principals and with those in school systems and universities who plan staff development programs for administrators. These chapters add up to an exciting challenge for us all. I want to thank Mary Hepburn and the other authors for their fine contribution to our field and for their patience as financial constraints delayed publication years beyond what was originally hoped.

A thank you is extended also to Jean Claugus and to Howard Mehlinger for drawing the Council's attention to the need to exercise leadership in democratizing schools. In 1974 and 1976 special committees were appointed to address this issue. The second committee, Ad Hoc Committee on Democratization of Schools, which was chaired by Mary Hepburn and had as members Edwin Fenton, Roger La Raus, Michael Radz, and Zada Koblas, developed the position statement which appears here, with the assistance of Theodore Kaltsounis. They also generated the idea for this Bulletin. The work of these individuals and of the authors has been extended further by the efforts of NCSS Citizenship Committee members who in many ways have assisted educators in improving citizenship education. To these people, and to all of you who are working daily to promote democracy through modeling justice, equity, inquiry, and participation, I am grateful.

Carole L. Hahn, *President*
National Council for the Social Studies

THE NCSS POSITION STATEMENT
ON DEMOCRATIZATION OF SCHOOLS

Democracy requires citizens who understand and are committed to its major tenets. Its capacity to survive rests upon the zeal and skill of each new generation of citizens. Schools have a main responsibility for preparing citizens who are knowledgeable about, prefer, and practice democracy.

Democracy implies freedom, but freedom must be balanced with responsibility. Acting democratically means pursuing personal goals while remaining respectful of the goals of others, exercising one's rights without infringing upon the rights of others, and tempering one's actions through considering the consequences to society if all acted in the same manner.

Becoming a democratic citizen requires more than an abstract understanding of democratic principles and practices. Behaving democratically is a way of life. It is not enough that schools preach democracy; they must practice it also and be able to instruct through modeling. What is taught from textbooks about the advantages of democracy should be exhibited within the school. Students should not be asked to accept the tenets of democracy on faith, but rather they should be assisted to develop commitments based on analysis and reason. Concurrently, the school experience should provide young people with an immediate example of a democratic system so that they can feel the effects of democracy.

While too often this does not happen, the school should be a microsociety and should reflect what is happening in the real world. Schools, like a society, have a system of justice and notions of equity. Some of the issues facing them are manifestations of problems confronting society as a whole. Examples of such problems are the need to eliminate racial injustice, crime, and inequalities of treatment toward men and women. Students need to feel a part of the system of justice, and they need to tackle the problems within the school setting in order to gain experience in the agony and frustration of democratic decision making.

Does democracy in school undermine authority? Certainly not. Exercising leadership and authority is not inconsistent with democracy, although styles of leadership not conforming to democratic principles clearly are. Capable teachers and administrators have found many opportunities to provide students with authentic democratic experience without relinquishing their positions of leadership or sacrificing respect. The most important ingredient for success in this area is making reason and evidence the major criteria for determining what is correct.

Approved by the NCSS Board of Directors
May 20, 1979

CHAPTER ONE

Introduction: Why We Should Be Concerned

Mary A. Hepburn & Michael A. Radz

If we should ask American social studies teachers if they are committed to the teaching of the principles of democracy based on the Constitution and the Bill of Rights, undoubtedly the great majority would readily respond in the affirmative. Many would explain how they teach about democracy in history, civics, and general social studies lessons year after year. Many teachers, guided and supported by subject supervisors and school administrators, do make a serious effort to teach democratic knowledge, skills, and values in the social studies curriculum. However, many educators remain unaware of the great numbers of opportunities for teaching these principles, skills, and values by means of school-life experiences.

The school as a microsociety and a miniature political system offers numerous opportunities for practicing and examining the application of democratic principles. Of course, the school is far from a perfect model of a democratic system. The bureaucratic framework in which it operates has been imposed externally by the school board and the larger community, and generally the framework is not subject to change by students or faculty. Nevertheless, the internal operation of the school offers numerous daily opportunities for participation and reflection. Internally, the character of a school's microsociety can range from highly autocratic to highly democratic, depending on the actions of administrators and teachers in the school at large and in individual classrooms.

The students, teachers, administrators, and staff who are part of a school's microsociety spend most of their waking hours in the school. Administrators set the pattern for interaction in the school, and teachers define these patterns in their classrooms; both have many opportunities to involve students in decision processes which help them learn about cooperation, justice, equal access, social control, and freedom and its democratic limits. Nevertheless, in many schools, democratic principles are taught only by class recitation, while the behavior of administrators and teachers, in their interactions with one another and with students, offers negative examples and little experience in democratic responsibility.

Consider, for example, the following newspaper report:

> Working hand in hand with school authorities, the local police chief and his men sealed off the 1,700-student high school and conducted a massive drug search.
>
> First they cut off the water to the school, then policemen with dogs started working their way through classrooms. Startled students sat at their desks for four hours with stern instructions that they not get up. Girls were ordered to leave their pocketbooks on top of the desks.
>
> Student by student, the dogs sniffed each of the pupils at the school, most of the time finding nothing suspicious. But not always. . . .
>
> Although school and police refuse to talk about it, some students reportedly undressed in a school office so they could be searched.
>
> When the detailed, lengthy search was over, no one had been arrested. Only two of the 1,700 students were suspended. . . .
>
> "If we go through another one [a search], we'll get more dogs," he [the police chief] said. "It was just too much for two dogs."
>
> Yet the police chief and school officials label the episode last month an unqualified success.
>
> The reason, he [the chief] says, is the psychological effect it has on students. "They [students] don't know what we'll be doing next," he said proudly. That's what has some people concerned.[1]

Could this, or does this, happen in your school? What does such an experience teach the students involved? How does this experience affect attitudes of community trust, political efficacy, respect for a system of justice? What kinds of role models are learned here? While teachers might not consider a police search of students in their school to be a learning activity, it is part of the school's curriculum—its hidden curriculum.

The view expressed throughout this book is that citizenship education must be viewed as more than the content of formal social studies courses. Realistically, it must be conceptualized as having three components: (1) the **hidden curriculum,** or informal learning experiences in the school; (2) the **societal curriculum,** or student learning experiences external to the school; as well as (3) the **formal curriculum,** or course of study.

The **hidden curriculum** is inextricably linked to the "climate" of the school. What is "school climate"? It is the atmosphere in which daily activities, major and minor, are conducted in the school. It reflects the ways in which people treat each other. It is the quality of life in the school and its general sociopolitical environment. The climate of the school, like the weather, does have an effect on its inhabitants. Unlike the weather, however, something can be done about a school's climate — especially by educators.

Urgently needed in many schools is an analysis of the hidden curriculum

---

[1]From "Juvenile Rights: Are They Being Abused by Cops," in *The Atlanta Journal and Constitution,* May 7, 1978.

and the climate which it is producing, followed by an effort to strengthen the link between the hidden curriculum and formal instruction. One significant way in which young citizens learn about such basic democratic values as rule of law, justice, human dignity, due process, and the responsible exercise of authority is by observing adult actors in the school setting. Often these living lessons do not coincide with what students are reading in history books and hearing in civics classes.

One method of working toward a democratic hidden curriculum is to seek a commitment from all groups in the school to make the school a laboratory for responsible democratic citizenship. Such a commitment can come about only after self-examination, discussion, and full awareness of the school's climate as a medium of education. This would mean that to a certain extent every adult in the school—not just social studies teachers— would be expected to contribute to citizenship education. A formal statement of the school's purposes in promoting democratic procedures and humane interpersonal relations, while clearly and fairly assigning responsibilities, could strengthen the commitment.

Teachers and administrators must also become aware of the **societal curriculum** as it interacts with schooling. It is well documented that children spend an enormous amount of time watching television. While there is no consensus as to the specific impact of television on citizenship behavior, it is obvious that television is an extremely powerful medium which transmits values both subtly and blatantly. In addition, there are radio programs, records, and periodicals addressed to the young audience. Role models abound; many are something less than positive. As members of a variety of youth organizations such as the Boy Scouts and Girl Scouts, 4-H, YMCA and YWCA, Little League, and church groups, students learn about power, authority, fairness, justice, human dignity, and other basic democratic values, as interpreted and practiced in these organizations. Not to be overlooked are informal peer groups and youth groups in which there is no adult supervision or direction. From these groups in early childhood, young students have already learned a great deal about political processes before they enter school.

Administrators and teachers in many schools have failed to come to grips with the fact that students, regardless of their grade level, are citizens. While the formal curriculum is aimed at preparing them for participation in a larger adult world sometime in the future, children are already practicing citizens of the school, home, and community. They have numerous first-hand opportunities to learn about rights and responsibilities. They have obligations and standards of conduct to consider, and numerous decisions to make about actions in their lives. Yet, many schools function as if citizenship is something that is bestowed at the conclusion of twelfth grade—as if a student is suddenly transformed at graduation into a "democratic citizen."

Increases in school violence, vandalism, and other crimes have caused administrators and teachers in some schools to react with extreme, oppressive measures. Yet, studies of schools suffering violence and crime show us that students are sensitive to the ways in which rules are made and enforced and that they tend to react negatively, sometimes violently, to perceptions of inequitable systems and unfair treatment.

In their daily experiences inside and outside of school, students gain lasting impressions of how democratic values are actually interpreted in American society. They form impressions of a system of justice which specifies means for dealing with infractions against rules and law. Yet, all too often in their schooling, they are presented with the hypocrisy of "do as we say, not as we do." Democratic experiences are presented as part of the adult future for which one prepares by reading and discussion, but not by practice.

The National Council for the Social Studies is committed to the teaching of the basic principles of democracy expressed in the Declaration of Independence and the Constitution. Awareness, analysis, and application of such principles cannot be left to chance. NCSS asserts that these basics of democratic education cannot be accomplished by the formal curriculum alone. Children need direct experience with responsible role models, the skills to analyze the messages they are receiving, and the self-esteem that allows them to function responsibly in the absence of direct supervision.

Our Committee, the Ad Hoc Committee on Democratization of the Schools, was appointed by President Howard Mehlinger in 1977 to review the subject, provide draft material to the Board of Directors for a position statement and prepare a publication. The Committee determined that the only realistic approach to democratic school education is one which takes into account both components of social-political education in the school—the formal school curriculum and the hidden school curriculum or environment of the school.

Other NCSS volumes have concerned changes in the formal curriculum. This volume focuses on the hidden curriculum which is subtly generated from social, political and academic expectations and interactions in the whole school and within individual classrooms. The Committee which produced this volume worked under the conviction that teachers and administrators must be aware of the learning climate they are creating. It is hoped that this publication will help to develop greater consciousness of the school setting and encourage practices which will strengthen democratic education in social studies classrooms and throughout the whole school.

CHAPTER TWO

Can Schools, Teachers, and Administrators Make a Difference? The Research Evidence

Mary A. Hepburn

A proposal to increase democratic education in the schools must offer teachers, administrators, and teacher educators more than exhortations and pronouncements. In an era of extensive research and analysis, we ask for more than opinions of what ought to be; we expect to examine evidence of what is possible. What does the research show? Can schools do more than teach *about* democracy? Can schools actually provide laboratory experiences in democracy? What happens when democratic principles are applied in schools and classrooms?

This chapter offers a summary of research evidence. Considerable research in the last several decades relates to questions of democratic schooling. Consequently, after a broad search, one must necessarily limit a review by selecting studies of American schools and classrooms which seem most appropriate. Most studies presented in this chapter were conducted in the last 20 years, but a few are older ones which deserve renewed attention.

Later chapters recommend and describe practical approaches to increasing democratic learning experiences. This research summary precedes the discussion of practical measures so that it may provide a useful knowledge base. Included are: (1) results of investigations which may suggest directions for action by teachers and administrators, and (2) explanatory or conceptual frameworks generated from research which gives us contexts for thinking about our actions.

The chapter is divided into three sections: (1) an introduction focusing on research related to the assumption that schools play a role in sociopolitical education; (2) a review of studies of the impact of the whole school, including its structure, size, activities, and political and social climate; and (3) a review of studies of classroom factors, including teachers' leadership styles, curriculum content, and teaching methods. The chapter divisions were determined by the focus of the studies, and are not meant to imply a clear separation. As is obvious to those who have worked in schools, the school and its classrooms do not operate independently of one another; they are inextricably interrelated.

Readers should keep in mind that the various studies reported do not provide all of the answers to questions related to democratic schooling. There are a number of missing links. Nevertheless, there is much evidence which will assist us in expanding our reflection on the NCSS Position Statement on Democratization of Schools.

Does the School Make a Difference?

Does the school affect political education of young people in a democratic society? In comparison with the family, peer groups, and the media, how much and what kinds of influence does the school exert? The political socialization research of the last twenty years leaves little doubt that school experiences *do* influence the political orientations of students. In a major study of the political attitudes of elementary school children in eight cities and four regions of the United States, Hess and Torney (1967) determined that the school is "the most important and effective instrument of political socialization in the United States" (p. 101). They found that early schooling reinforces the young child's attachment to the nation and trust in political authority figures. Schools shape children's regard for law and law enforcement and the conviction that citizens should participate by voting. Hess and Torney concluded that while the family shapes basic loyalties, "the school apparently plays the largest part in teaching attitudes, conceptions, and beliefs about the operation of the political system." The school provides "content, information, and concepts," adding to early attitudes learned at home (p. 217).

Greenstein (1967), in a study of elementary students in New Haven, Connecticut, observed that many political orientations are learned by American children without deliberate instruction and that learning goes on unnoticed, especially in the early years, when students are less likely to question what they experience in school. The notion that in the early grades schooling effectively interacts with family training to mold the political attitudes of children was further supported by Torney (1970). From interviews with both elementary and secondary students, she concluded that schooling influences the political attitudes of students in two ways: (1) by developing expectations of the authority system which are then transferred to other institutions, and (2) by cognitive development which broadens students' perspectives. Torney determined that the years immediately preceding high school are crucial for attitude development.

On the other hand, a study of a large national probability sample in the late sixties has been widely cited as evidence that the civics education curriculum in high schools is ineffective (Langton and Jennings, 1968). It examined the relationship between the number of civics courses taken and the political attitudes and knowledge of high school students and reported that the curriculum had only a very weak influence. However, recent criticisms of the validity of the measurement of political attitudes (Stentz and Lambert, 1977) and political knowledge (Hepburn, 1980) indicate that the results of the Langton and Jennings study must be viewed with serious reservations.

In an international study of civic education in ten democratic countries, Torney, Oppenheim, and Farnen (1975) found that in countries where schools stressed nationalistic and patriotic ritual or traditional recitation, students were less knowledgeable about and exhibited less support for democratic values, *but* demonstrated a higher interest in political participation. They concluded that, in addition to conscious, deliberate efforts in classes to teach democratic values and basic political knowledge, many subtle unintentional processes are at work in the schools which also transmit political concepts and values.

In a review of recent political socialization research, Ehman (1980) determined that in comparison to other agents of socialization, such as the family and the media, schools do play an important role in political education. He concluded, however, that "schooling is relatively more important in influencing political knowledge than political attitudes" (p. 113). It should be noted that Ehman's generalization refers mainly to studies of the formal school curriculum, including the Langton and Jennings study criticized above. Additional evidence in his review indicates that school and classroom climate have considerable influence on student political attitudes.

A study utilizing extensive data from nationwide samples of the National Assessment of Educational Progress (Mullis, 1978) compared effects of home, school, and community variables and produced strong support for the argument that the schools play a *major* role in shaping both political knowledge and attitudes. Mullis reported that the direct effect of the school on political knowledge was greater than the direct effect of home. The direct effect of the school on sociopolitical attitudes was also greater than the direct effects of the home. "School effects" included several formal or deliberate factors in political education, such as number of courses and instruction which teaches how to acquire information and analyze alternatives, but it also included measures of school climate. When both indirect and direct effects were considered, the total influence of the home was only slightly greater than the influence of the school. This comparative analysis reveals the high relative effect of school variables and suggests the importance of the school's role in the sociopolitical education of students in the United States.

Overall, the weight of evidence points to schools and schooling as significant in the political education of young citizens in the United States. The influencing factors are not only the obvious ones—curriculum, course work, and content, but also the more subtle features of a school which make up its social and political environments, or "climate."

THE WHOLE SCHOOL

Halpin and Croft (1963) carried out pioneering research which provided the extensive empirical evidence that schools do have differing climates which influence the performance of the people within them. Hypothesizing that the climate of social interaction in the school is to school organization what personality is to the individual, Halpin and Croft sought to map school climates by describing specific characteristics of the social interaction between the principal and the teachers.

The data were obtained from questionnaires administered to teachers and principals. Items of the Organizational Climate Description Question- naire were based on observed school situations and previous research. The questionnaire was carefully developed, pilot-tested, and reduced to the 150 most effective items. Items for teachers tested four areas: (1) *disen- gagement,* the tendency just to go through the motions and not be involved; (2) *hindrance,* the feeling of being burdened with busy work by the principal; (3) *esprit,* morale, or a feeling of accomplishment on the job; and (4) *intimacy,* the extent of friendly social relations which teachers enjoyed with each other. Items regarding the principal tested: (1) *aloofness*, the degree of distance which the principal maintained from the staff; (2) *production emphasis,* the amount of direction and closeness of supervision of staff; (3) *trust,* the efforts to motivate and move the staff; and (4) *consideration*, the degree to which teachers were treated humanely and with kindness.

From the 71 elementary schools in their study, Halpin and Croft identi- fied six organizational climates ranging from open, democratic environ- ments, where teachers and principal worked well together, to closed, oppressive social environments, where both teachers and principal were dissatisfied with the school. Results of the research provide practical infor- mation by which teachers and principals can review the climate of their own schools.

School Size and Climate

A study which focused on students rather than administrators or teachers examined the various school "behavior settings" in which students experi- ence schooling and investigated the relationship of student participation to school size (Barker and Gump, 1965). High schools of different sizes were studied in terms of the contents or settings for student activities. Some academic and many extracurricular settings were examined. It was found that there were fewer varieties of formal educational settings and extra-curricular settings in small schools. However, in larger schools, students *participated* in fewer classes and in less varieties of classes than in smaller schools. Likewise, the average number and kind of extracurricular activities engaged in by students was greater in the smaller high schools.

A subsequent study (Kleinert, 1969) reinforced the findings of the study by Barker and Gump. The relationship between high school size and student participation in extracurricular activities was examined in 63 high schools ranging in size from 87 to 3,068 students. Student participation showed a strong negative relationship to school size with the decline in participation greatest at 600 or more students. The research concluded that the larger the school, the less it provides students with opportunities to "take initiative, to enjoy recognition, to exercise leadership."

The negative relationship between school size and student participation suggests that smaller high schools or semiautonomous units within larger high schools may help to democratize schools by increasing participation and encouraging more varied activities. In large high schools that cannot be reorganized or reduced in size, Kleinert has recommended that opportunities for student participation could be created by having several football teams, several bands, several drama groups, etc.

A more recent study lends support to the notion that smaller administrative units within larger schools may increase their potential for providing a democratic climate. The political attitudes of students in a large comprehensive high school of 4,000 students were compared with the political attitudes of students in the 250-student alternative school contained within the larger school (Metzger and Barr, 1978). Students in the alternative school believed that they had a greater access to information, more influence on school decision-making, and more opportunities for participation in forming school policy. On the basis of these differences, the researchers determined that the two schools offered significantly different political systems. Students in the smaller alternative school demonstrated more positive school-related political attitudes and more positive society-related political attitudes.

Student Attitudes Toward the School's Authority Structure

How do students perceive and react to the authority structure of their schools? Several studies suggest that students become alienated from their school when they have little input into school goals, rules, or decisions. High school students' feelings of powerlessness and alienation were found to be positively related to "custodial" school control, which is rigid and highly regulated in comparison to more cooperative "humanistic" control, which emphasizes self-discipline (Rafeledes and Hoy, 1971). Apparently, high school students are conscious of the power structure in their school. In a comparison of students' perceptions of the distribution of power in ten high schools, Wittes (1972) found significant between-school differences in student perceptions of the decision-making structure and a clear relationship between students' sense of personal power and the actual power structure in the school.

In a study probing several dimensions of the political attitudes of 920 students in third, eighth, and twelfth grades, Hepburn and Napier (1982-83), using a 48-item attitude instrument, found that on the surface students showed increasingly positive attitudes toward political participation and institutions as they progressed through school. However, subtest analysis revealed that by the eighth grade there was a disaffection in some political attitude dimensions.

While positive attitudes toward *public* political participation persisted across the grades, a remarkable "self/other" dichotomy manifested itself in attitudes toward *school* political participation by the eighth grade and continued into the twelfth. A similar, but less dramatic fragmentation of attitudes toward political institutions was found. Older students expressed disillusionment with the ways in which political institutions work for them personally. It was also evident that among the eighth and twelfth graders there was an "others-should-but-I-would-not" view of school political participation. The researchers projected that two levels of learning were affecting student attitudes: the formal civics curriculum, which teaches positive attitudes *about* the ideals of political participation in their future adult lives; and the "hidden" curriculum, which inculcates skepticism and even cynicism in regard to the responsiveness of political institutions— especially the school.

In an assessment of the attitudes of high school students toward school governance, a study by Serow and Strike (1978) indicated that students do not desire *unlimited* influence on school policy. The students from 19 high schools accepted the school administration as the ultimate arbiter of peer conflicts and supported administrative interference which would protect students from physical or psychological injury. On the other hand, they objected to administrators who over-centralize authority and "pull rank" on them, as well as administrators who assume unrestricted power *in loco parentis* in political and moral matters.

Middle school students also express feelings of alienation toward schools when they perceive that teachers and administrators exert excessive authority. In a study of seven middle schools, students from schools where administrators and teachers determined all of the goals showed stronger feelings of powerlessness, isolation, and alienation than students from schools where students had some input into school and classroom goals (Dillon and Grout, 1976).

The vast national study undertaken by the National Institute of Education sought to determine the characteristics associated with greater or less crime and violence in schools (Boesel, 1978). Violence and crime in large city schools had generated concern of such proportions in the mid seventies that Congress called for research into the seriousness of the problem and descriptive data which would suggest policy initiatives alleviating the problem. One project of the three-phase study known as the Safe Schools Study consisted of on-site surveys of a representative national sample of 642 public junior and senior high schools (Boesel, Chapter 5). A written questionnaire was administered to students, teachers, and principals to collect data on school characteristics and reports of violent and/or criminal incidents which had occurred in school within a one-month period. Data scales were constructed to measure rule enforcement, sense of internal school control, fairness of school environment, school governance, relevance of school subjects, and amount of violence.

Some interesting relationships between characteristics of the school climate and organization and rates of school violence and crime were reported. A powerful predictor of school crime was the type—not the degree—of school discipline. Highly disciplined schools were not necessarily associated with student rebellion and discontent. Rather, highly disciplined schools, which also had a respected and efficient principal, a relatively high degree of teacher satisfaction, and consistent disciplinary policies perceived by the students to be enforced fairly, were associated with low rates of crime and violence. Fairness appeared to be an important factor. In schools where students perceived that discipline and rules were arbitrary and unfairly applied, there were higher rates of violence and property damage. The presence of school government organizations was not necessarily associated with lower crime. On the other hand, student perceptions that they had no internal control and could not influence what happened to them in school was related to greater violence and crime. Perceptions of a realistic and fairly administered academic reward system were also related to better student behavior in the schools. Besides providing a wealth of descriptive data, the Safe Schools Study heightens our awareness of the need to examine multiple factors as we attempt to learn more about the influences on and the effects of school climate.

From written discussions of incidents of school conflict obtained from 6,700 junior and senior high school students, Richards and DeCecco (1975) determined that students perceive schools as authoritarian institutions when conflict is customarily resolved by the use of force. The researchers assessed whether students applied democratic concepts of civic participation to incidents of school conflict and whether they perceived alternative solutions to conflicts. Over half of the incidents dealt with individual rights or self-governance. In 55 percent of the incidents, conflict was resolved by the authority, and in nearly 82 percent, no alternative means of resolving the conflict was offered by students. Only 17 percent mentioned "negotiation" as a means of settling an issue. The researchers concluded that school experiences teach students that problems should be solved by the unilateral decision of authorities rather than by more democratic means which could provide students with opportunities for studying due process, making decisions, and taking responsibility for those decisions.

The Effects of Participation

The implication of much of the above research is that a school climate which encourages student input and perceptions of fair treatment and due process will better educate students for democratic citizenship. What evidence do we have on the effects of participation?

Evidently, participation in school extracurricular activities contributes to the development of democratic political attitudes. In a study of the attitudes and activities of high school sophomores and seniors, Ziblatt (1970) found that the more students participated in extracurricular activities, the greater were their feelings of social integration and social trust and the more positive were their attitudes toward politics. Investigating the relationship of feelings of powerlessness to certain school and social variables, Burbach (1972) found that high school students generally felt more powerless in the high school than in society at large. However, students who held school offices felt more in control of events. Generally, the number of extracurricular activities, grade-point average, and college aspirations were inversely related to feelings of powerlessness in regard to school and to the society. On the other hand, Merelman (1971), comparing the effects of two different school climates, reported only a tenuous link between the democratic attitudes of students and educational factors including school governance activities.

Ehman and Gillespie (1975) conceptualized schools as micropolitical systems, defined *a priori* types of schools, and tested the types with data from 13 high schools. Four types of schools were conceptualized: (1) **elite,** where administrators have a monopoly on participation, leadership, communication, and influence in the school, and decisions are enforced by coercion; (2) **bureaucratic,** where administrators and teachers dominate decision-making, and position or power is the basis of influence; (3) **coalition,** where various groups participate in the system and bargain over issues which arise, and no one group dominates continually; and (4)

participant, where the students have a major role in the decisions made and are able to assume leadership in a system which seeks consensus.

A dominant bureaucratic pattern was found in all 13 schools, but within this basic bureaucratic type, elite, participant, and coalition characteristics were identified. School organization and operations apparently influenced political student attitudes of political efficacy, political trust, and social integration. Students gave the highest ratings to student government groups as the formal organizations which made decisions of most importance to them. Student attitudes toward the school political system were highly related to societal political attitudes. Students who showed high levels of school interest and confidence also showed high levels of general political interest and confidence, suggesting to the researchers that political attitudes formed from school experiences are generalized outward to the larger society.

A moral development approach to democratic school governance based on Kohlberg's idea of the "just community" is reported in a descriptive account of the Cluster School (Wasserman, 1980; Wasserman and Garrod, 1982). In the mid seventies, a group of parents, teachers, and students gained permission to set up the Cluster School as an alternative high school within Cambridge (Massachusetts) High and Latin School, a large, inner city high school. While students and staff had to operate within the existing fundamental local and state school regulations, they did have a large measure of autonomy in relation to the larger school. Issues of interpretation and enforcement of rules were dealt with in large community meetings and with smaller representative bodies in terms of moral dilemmas. The core curriculum which was taught in social studies and English classes focused on moral discussions of school governance issues and related issues in society. It was theorized that a school atmosphere which maximized student opportunities to voice opinions and to make group decisions would promote moral growth and more responsible action which would carry over to the larger society. (See Chapter Three for a fuller description of the school as a "just community".)

Evidently a systematic qualitative evaluation of the Cluster School was not conducted. However, from observations recorded by a staff participant (Wasserman, 1980), it was concluded that under the participant governance structure of the just community, students developed skills in resolving issues of fairness and in their relationships with staff and other students they felt more respect and trust.

Making Use of Research:
A Typology of School Climates

The research on the climate of schools has produced explanatory frameworks which can be of practical value to administrators and teachers who seek to understand how they influence the climate of a school. Such conceptual or explanatory frameworks can help personnel as they review their schools and consider ways in which to create a better learning environment for democratic citizenship.

The research conducted by Halpin and Croft (1963) offers a useful framework in which to examine interactions of administrators and teachers. Their investigation provided no information about effects on students, but it did reveal how different types of climates develop from the differing types of day-to-day working behaviors of the principal and teachers. The six types of school climate were conceptualized along a continuum from "closed" to "open" (Figure 1).

Figure 1.   Types of School Climates

Closed	Paternal	Familiar	Controlled	Autonomous	Open

Closed Climate. Characterized by very closed and non-genuine relationships between principal and teachers.

Teachers obtain little satisfaction from their work; fail to accomplish much; have a low morale; have a high turnover rate; may have some friendly relations with colleagues, but generally have a low *esprit de corps;* and achieve mainly "housekeeping" work, such as required reports.

Principal is highly aloof and impersonal; stresses hard work and emphasizes production, but is usually not a model worker; sets down arbitrary rules; fails to provide adequate leadership; and is inconsiderate of the social needs of the teachers, who tend to regard him or her as a phony.

Paternal Climate. Characterized by closed and generally non-genuine relationships, with the principal as a persistent watchdog.

Teachers are split into factions; do not work well together; are not burdened by reports and busy work (because principal does them), but have few responsibilities; gain inadequate satisfaction from their work; and do not enjoy friendly relations with each other.

Principal is continually checking, prying, monitoring, and intruding in all areas; does not let teachers lead or make decisions; wants to know everything; fails to motivate teachers; and tends to be over-solicitous in matters of personal consideration, rather than genuinely concerned.

Familiar Climate. Characterized by conspicuous friendliness of teachers and administrators, but lack of direction toward achievement of school goals.

Teachers are friendly with each other and fairly relaxed in their working environment; their morale derives from social satisfaction, rather than a sense of accomplishment; they feel that little is required of them; and they perceive the principal as a "good guy" rather than a leader.

Principal wants to be liked by everybody; offers little direction, little guidance, and few rules; does not emphasize production or encourage it; and is highly considerate of the teachers personally, but fails to motivate them to define or accomplish goals professionally.

Controlled Climate. Characterized by pressure for achievement and hard work. However, the climate is more "open" than "closed."

Teachers are highly task-oriented, but have much busy work and paperwork to do; have little feeling or camaraderie and few social relations, but do obtain job satisfaction from task accomplishment.

Principal is domineering, directive, and inflexible; delegates few responsibilities; remains aloof from teachers; requires excessive paperwork; centers power in the principal's office and determines both ends and means; has little consideration for personal social needs of teachers.

Autonomous Climate. Characterized by freedom of teachers to develop their own internal leadership patterns.

Teachers have a strong *esprit de corps* and good social relations; are involved in their work and achieve their goals; have little hindrance from administrative paperwork; and make many middle-level decisions about use of supplies, etc., among themselves.

Principal is genuine; but businesslike and quite aloof; sets an example by working hard; is flexible, but provides leadership and control; sets up guidelines which teachers can follow and then with a minimum of monitoring allows them to set their own pace; and is considerate of teachers.

Open Climate. Characterized by teachers and administrators working well together to accomplish their goals.

Teachers work well together, without bickering; are not burdened by routine busy work, but are assisted by the principal in accomplishing their objectives; are highly motivated to work and overcome difficulties; enjoy considerable job satisfaction; and are proud of the school.

Principal is genuine, in that personality and leadership role are well integrated; sets an example of hard work; can criticize or praise in a considerate manner; is not aloof, but involved, and can show compassion while providing clear direction; allows appropriate leadership to emerge from teachers; and does not need to monitor them closely for them to be highly productive.

Compare these types to your school. Copies of the typology might be distributed in a faculty meeting for discussion. These classifications show the principal as the pivotal individual in the shaping of the climate of the whole school. The principal is in the key leadership position and can minimize suspicion, lack of interest, and other unproductive attitudes, while promoting democratic organization and good working relationships. Further, the more open and democratic school environment tends to be a more efficient and more enjoyable place for teachers to work, and, as suggested by other more recent studies, it provides a better setting for learning than does the closed school environment. The typology can be used as the context for motivating faculty and administrators to improve school climate.

THE CLASSROOM

The climate of the classroom and its influence on the performance and attitudes of students have long interested educational and psychological researchers. Efforts to measure and experiment with classroom climate date back nearly fifty years. The research over the years, however, shows notable changes in focus and conceptualization.

The Teacher's Leadership Style

In the late thirties, at a time when American interest in understanding and preserving democratic group relationships was intensified by the anti-democratic actions of Fascist regimes in Europe, Lewin, Lippitt and White conducted the first major studies of the effects of the social climate of the classroom. They focused their studies on the teacher as climate maker. Because their classic research is of direct consequence to the topic of democratic schooling and because it is widely cited, but seldom described, it is reviewed here in some detail.

Lewin, Lippett, and White studied the social climate produced by three types of classroom leadership—**democratic, autocratic,** and **laissez-faire** (Lewin, 1938; Lewin, Lippett, and White, 1939; White and Lippett, 1960). The classroom groups in the main experiment were made up of fifth-grade boys from schools in a middle-sized Midwestern city who had volunteered for membership in clubs. The clubs were organized ostensibly to carry on such projects as constructing model airplanes, theatrical masks, or clubroom furniture. On the basis of sociometric data obtained from the schools, students were assigned to four roughly equivalent groups. Group loyalty was stimulated by allowing each group to choose a club name and decorate its own clubroom.

Each group had an adult male leader. The leader created the climate in each group by his leadership behavior. The different types of leaders were rotated after several weeks so that the same students could be studied in different classroom climates. The clubs met through three six-week periods. Teams of observers took notes on leader behavior and student behavior throughout the experiment.

The **autocratic** leader dictated all policy and gave step-by-step directions on what was to be done and by whom on each club project, to the extent that students in this group often did not know future steps. The leader decided which students would be allowed to work together. When he expressed praise or criticism, it was in personal terms and in a non-objective, judgmental manner.

In the **democratic** group, policies were determined by group discussion and group decision, with the leader giving only general guidance and some assistance. He aided the group in defining overall goals and suggested alternative procedures, but urged members of the group to make their own decisions. Group members divided the tasks and were generally free to work with whomever they wished. The leader attempted to be objective when praising or criticizing the students and acted as a group member, rather than a boss, by providing information and suggestions, but leaving the responsibility for carrying out cooperative projects to the students.

The **laissez-faire** climate was not originally planned in the experiments but emerged in an earlier study when one of the adult leaders who attempted democratic leadership was unsuccessful. The members of this group lapsed into extremely individualistic and uncooperative behavior which finally declined into anarchy. The leader offered no guidance in setting goals, making decisions, or selecting work partners. The laissez-faire's leader supplied information only when asked, provided no work assistance, and did not praise or criticize. In the laissez-faire climate, individual students were free to determine their goals and activities without concern for the group.

Observations showed that under *autocratic* leadership, group behavior was generally submissive. Students were motivated to work on their projects only when the leader was present. When the leader was watching and told students specifically what to do, they worked efficiently, but when he left the room, work ceased or slowed. There was greater tension and hostility among students in the autocratic climate, and they tended to direct their hostility at one person. There was less cooperation among members, and the group tended to be unstable.

Students who experienced *democratic* leadership were more efficient and successful in accomplishing their goals. They were more cohesive as a group, and they expressed a sense of group accomplishment in the use of "we" to refer to their actions. They were less apathetic than the group in the autocratic situation and more inclined to express their individual views in meetings. The democratic climate also stimulated more objective exchange of criticism. Overall, they demonstrated a greater sense of fairness and less concern over status than the other groups.

Under *laissez-faire* leadership, the students attempted some group activity but quickly lapsed into disruptive behavior. Members of the group became aggressive toward each other—a change which was attributed to the absence of a respected adult, idleness, and frustration over their lack of accomplishment. The *laissez-faire* group failed to achieve their work goals. Observers noted that students who were disruptive in this climate tended to work on tasks by teams when in the democratic climate. Further, in the *laissez-faire* group only one or two students would clean up after a session, whereas in a democratic climate the boys readily worked together to clean the clubroom. In summary, the democratic classroom climate was not only more productive, but there were many indications that it was more satisfying to its members than either the *laissez-faire* or the autocratic climate.

Other Behavioral Factors of the Teacher's Leadership

Subsequent studies have attempted to identify additional behavioral factors of the teacher's style of leadership which contribute to the development of an open or democratic classroom climate. First- and fifth-grade classrooms where teachers were concerned with student compliance with authority and rules have been compared to more open classrooms where teacher-student relations were conducted on a person-to-person basis. The study found that the students who experienced the open climate chose more democratic methods to resolve conflicts and were less dependent and submissive than their counterparts in the more authoritarian classes (Allman-Snyder et al., 1975).

Hawley (1977) examined the degree to which the teacher's respect for students' ideas and encouragement of expression increase tolerance for and interest in the views of other students. A positive relationship was reported in this study of fifth-grade classes. However, students' perceptions of the classroom climate were more closely linked to the teacher's attitudes than to his or her actual teaching style. Therefore, Hawley concluded that the teacher's approval of and provision for open interaction was more influential than the actual interaction behaviors.

The conceptualization of classroom climate was broadened by Fowlkes (1976), who focused on student needs and the extent to which these needs are satisfied by decision structures provided by teachers. She theorized that the more satisfied students are with the way decisions are made in the classroom, the more trust they will have in the teacher as an authority, and that the trust developed in the classroom will be generalized to government authorities. In exploratory research with high school classes, she tested the degree to which student needs for participation in classroom decisions matched their perception of actual involvement. The need to participate was least satisfied in areas of decision-making involving the choice of class topics and the making of class rules. While students wanted to participate more in choosing the topics discussed and in making rules, they preferred that grading be the teacher's responsibility. They expressed mixed views on who should choose learning strategies and who should determine punishments. Additional results indicated that trust in the teacher was a source of general political trust, which suggests for our purposes that trust in the teacher is a necessary component of democratic schooling.

The credibility of the leader or teacher was found to be essential to the process of producing attitude changes in a group, and the credibility of the teacher is of particular significance for productivity in an open classroom environment (Powell, 1965). In secondary social studies classes, Goldenson (1978) found that students who rated teachers high on credibility (well liked, expert on the subject, high prestige) were more likely to have made positive political attitude changes than students who rated teachers low on credibility.

Content and Teaching Methods

Thus far in this review, we have considered the less formal factors of personal interaction which can contribute to a democratic classroom climate. Numerous studies suggest ways in which the formal content of social studies courses and the teaching methods employed can also play a role in the democratization of learning experiences.

An assessment of students' opinions about the content and methods of the government and civics instruction which they received in their high schools was conducted by Remy (1972). The national sample was a selective group of mostly white, college-bound, middle-class high school seniors. On written questionnaires 40 to 60 percent complained that fundamentals of government were overemphasized; little attention was given to comparative political systems or controversial issues; new knowledge from political science was not included; content was not realistic; and courses failed to offer practical participatory skills, critical thinking skills, and examinations of political values. A majority of the students expressed a desire to participate in class political discussions and in school political activities. Generally, this relatively advantaged group of seniors was dissatisfied with the content, materials, and methods used in their civic education courses.

A Title IV curriculum project designed to improve the content and outcomes of political/citizenship education tested an improvement model which conceptualizes ;the school as a system with interrelated components which influence learning (Hepburn and Napier, 1982, 1982–83). The project focused on classroom teachers as change agents providing them with five types of system support: an in-service political education program for teachers, an education program for administrators, specific learning objectives, mobilization of community resources, and provision of supplemental instructional media. Curriculum materials emphasized analytical and participation skills and six content areas of political knowledge—democratic principles, national government, state and local government, politics, law and individual rights, and global affairs. The model proved effective as measured by pre-tests and post-tests of student citizenship knowledge and political attitudes in ten secondary social studies classes and 17 elementary classes compared to match control classes.

Controversial Issues

Infusing controversial issues into social studies content has been proposed as a means of strengthening student decision-making skills, broadening participation in the classroom, and improving democratic political attitudes. Studies of the effects of using controversial issues in high school social studies courses by Ehman (1969, 1977) indicated that increased controversial content had a positive effect on students' attitudes toward citizen duty, political participation, and political efficacy (1969), as well as their political trust, social integration, and political interest (1977), if the teacher allowed open expression and promoted an open classroom climate. The research further showed that the use of controversial issues as social studies content in a closed environment produced negative attitudes, especially in black students.

Long and Long (1975) reported that students who participated in discussion of controversial issues in high school social studies classes expressed more positive perceptions of the teachers, courses, and the school. They did not, however, find a positive correlation between discussions of controversy and attitudes of political efficacy and tolerance. These researchers utilized student data solely, and although they assessed perceptions of the teachers' willingness to use controversial issues in the classroom, they did not attempt to measure the openness of the classroom climate.

Controversial issues apparently can be used in moral reasoning strategies to develop stronger democratic values. Lockwood (1975, 1978) investigated the link between controversial public policy issues and real-life moral dilemmas in interviews with eighth and eleventh graders and found a moderate positive association. Discussion of the moral dilemmas in daily life with sixth-grade students was found by Dozier (1974) to reduce racial prejudice significantly, while promoting moral development. Discussions of everyday classroom dilemmas with fifth-grade students was found to be effective in promoting cooperative interaction and moral development (Rundle, 1977; Mosher, 1980).

Generally, the introduction of controversial issues alone is not adequate to strengthen democratic attitudes. A democratic classroom climate, normative or values-oriented or dilemma-oriented teaching approaches, and a focus on real-life student issues all appear to be contributing factors.

Cooperative and Competitive Strategies

The use of teams, gámes, and tournaments (TGT) in class review activities appears to offer another means of increasing the democratic climate in the classroom. These teaching strategies combine group cooperation and team competition as a means of promoting mutual concern among students, positive attitudes toward schooling and achievement, and a tolerance and appreciation of the natural diversities of students. Students are organized into several teams, each including students of diverse achievement levels, race, and sex. The teams have regular practice sessions during which peer tutors prepare teammates for the weekly tournament by reviewing the knowledge and skills which were taught on previous days through regular teaching methods. For the weekly tournaments, students are assigned to a tournament table to compete individually in prepared review games against students from other teams who are roughly comparable in achievement. At the conclusion of the tournament, points scored by students at the tournament table are tallied with the scores of their teammates, each from other tables. This system of reward interdependence is aimed at encouraging students to help each other learn in an effort to compete effectively in the weekly tournament against other teams.

A series of experiments with TGT in the classroom (see DeVries and Slavin, 1978, and Slavin, 1980, for summaries) have been generally effective in improving mutual concern among students, improving relationships between black, white, and Mexican-American students and, in some cases, improving students' self-esteem and attitudes toward school (Slavin, 1980). TGT has been less successful in increasing academic achievement in social studies than in basic mathematics, language arts, and reading vocabulary instruction. It appears, however, that this teaching technique can bring about greater group self-control, while maintaining the same level of achievement, in social studies classes (O'Neill, 1980).

Another perspective on student interaction in the classroom was generated from an analysis of results of over 122 studies which compared the effects of a variety of cooperative, competitive, and individualistic instructional strategies on student achievement and attitudes (Johnson, 1981). The synthesis implies avenues for democratizing the classroom while promoting achievement. Specific recommendations are that teachers structure cooperative learning goals in their classroom instruction and that they utilize and manage controversies to encourage student-to-student inter-action, cooperative learning experiences, and constructive controversy. (In Chapter 4, VanSickle discusses teaching approaches aimed at reducing classroom status effects and promoting cooperation across ability, racial, and social groups.)

Encouraging Student Expression

Student-initiated interaction is a teaching approach which has been found to relate positively to student feelings of political efficacy and negatively to political cynicism (Ponder and Button, 1975). Positive effects upon attitude were especially prevalent among white females in twelfth grade govern-ment classes which were composed of black, white, and Mexican-American students. In a class environment where student-initiated interaction was encouraged, student initiations of discussion increased, especially among black students.

A major cross-national comparative study of students from ten countries including the U.S. (Torney, et. al., 1975) suggests the importance of student expression. Attitudes of support for democratic values, support for national government, and interest in political discussion and participation were surveyed in addition to student civic knowledge. From data of nine of the countries surveyed, it was concluded that the one school variable that seemed to have positive effects on the measured outcomes was a classroom climate in which students are encouraged to express their opinions.

Instructional strategies which actively involve high school students in community service activities or political campaigns were studied by Jones (1975), who reported that this method of teaching was effective in increas-ing political efficacy and political participation skills, but did not increase favorable attitudes toward political processes and public officials.

An experiment which examined several classroom factors, including community involvement, was conducted by Goldenson (1978), who com-pared attitude changes in classes where civil liberties were taught in a traditional, teacher-centered manner to more open classes where students interacted with community resource people and discussed conflict issues and value perspectives. Positive attitude changes were found in nearly 20 percent more of the experimental students than the control students. Goldenson's conclusion is one implied throughout much of the research on classroom climate: three factors—the teacher's leadership characteristics, the teaching method, and the course content—all interact to influence the democratic attitudes of students.

The Restrained Climate Makers

The political climate of the classroom is bound to be influenced by teachers' attitudes, and there has been persistent evidence that teachers themselves are influenced by the climate of the educational institutions of which they are a part. Schools must attempt to serve the educational needs of people from a variety of social and economic backgrounds. Probably to avoid criticism by local interest groups and possibly to avoid undermining their own authority, teachers have tended to shy away from discussion of political subjects in the classroom. In the 1930s, Beale (1936) reported numerous cases of prohibition of political discussion in social studies classrooms and described restrictions on teachers' political participation away from school. Beyond the restraints of school policy, Beale noted a teacher tendency toward self-imposed restraints.

Thirty years later, in a study of the political orientations of Oregon high school teachers, Zeigler (1966) measured *sanction-proneness,* the perception of and sensitivity to inhibiting forces in the school system and community. He found that social studies teachers tended to be more sanction-prone than teachers of other subjects. Similar influences of the professional environment were reported: (1) New York social studies teachers, who felt that expectations of them as teachers negatively influenced their personal political activities as democratic citizens (Godward, 1963); (2) Florida social studies teachers' perceptions of the prohibitions which school policy imposed on teaching about political issues greatly exceeded actual restrictions (Hepburn, 1969); (3) Kansas social studies teachers with six years or less of experience who had social science degrees were more supportive of classroom expression on political topics than those with degrees in education or physical education, but the difference diminished as teaching experience increased (Ungs, 1968). Over the years, it appears that professionally-related inhibitions, often self-imposed, have contributed to timidity on the part of teachers and have created a "do as I say, not as I do" atmosphere for citizenship education. As teachers in some regions have become better organized professionally and politically, these inhibitions have perhaps declined. Research is needed to assess attitudes of the 80s.

Making Use of Research: A Context for Self-Review

A conceptual framework which can assist us in reviewing the effects of curriculum and instruction on democratic values is found in an analysis of how the educational system transmits political values, by Jaros (1969). In Jaros's analysis, there are three basic citizen values which are influenced by the educational system: (1) **participatory values,** which are norms about the desirability and obligation to participate personally in civic affairs, including feelings about the ability to obtain fair treatment by policy administrators; (2) **regime-level substantive values,** which include not only feelings of loyalty and patriotism, but also feelings about who should have access to the political decision-making process; and (3) **issue values,** which are feelings in regard to specific current conflict issues over public policy.

In an effort to clarify the ways in which the educational process influences American political values, Jaros delineated six processes through which schools shape students' political attitudes:

(1) Participatory classroom milieus—the degree to which the classroom involves students and allows them to express their views.

(2) Curricular content—the effect of the formal educational program which is aimed at teaching political knowledge and values.

(3) Curricular content mediated by "effective" teachers—the effects of such qualities as the teacher's warmth, organization, and stimulation interacting with content to produce attitude changes.

(4) Teachers' overt expression of their own values in the classroom—the extent to which personal values of teachers are transmitted in the classroom.

(5) Value expression outside of class—impressions gained by students from school personnel in informal, extracurricular settings where teachers may express their views.

(6) Teachers as models for political values—effects of the overall behavior of teachers which lead students to emulate them.

Another variable which Jaros calls "communications processes" pervades all of the six areas of influence. It refers to the style of communication, the size of classroom groups, and the extent of appeal to different levels of students.

In this conceptualization, it is evident that the emphasis is on teachers. Teachers are seen as the individuals who have the kind of daily contact and direct interaction with students which can develop lasting impresssions. The conceptual framework offers teachers a context for examining both the obvious and the subtle ways in which they shape the political values of students. By reviewing professional and personal behavior in each of these six processes, teachers can estimate in what ways and to what degree they are having an influence on the political attitudes of their students.

SUMMARY

The research in education and political socialization generally supports the conclusion that democratic experiences in the school and the classroom can contribute to the knowledge, skills, and attitudes essential to democratic citizenship. There are exceptions in the research literature, but the preponderant evidence indicates that:

(1) The school does play an important role in the political/citizenship education of young Americans, and, together with home and society, it shapes many student attitudes related to democratic principles. The factors which influence students include both the formal features of planned learning activities and the more subtle, informal features of the general climate of school and classrooms.

(2) The school climate is greatly influenced by the principal and other administrators through the organizational framework which is established and the ways in which teachers and students are treated.

(a) The degree of openness of principal-teacher interactions shapes the climate of the school and the effectiveness of the staff. A more open, democratic school environment tends to encourage productivity and positive attitudes of teachers.

(b) When principals and other administrators initiate the mechanisms which encourage student participation in certain areas of decision-making such as school justice systems and school governance, these experiences help to build positive student attitudes in regard to political trust and political participation.

(3) Small high schools or large high schools containing semiautonomous units provide the greatest opportunities for student participation in extracurricular activities and school decision-making, thus generating more positive political attitudes.

(4) Students are clearly aware of the extent to which their schools are run autocratically or democratically, and they express cynicism, alienation, powerlessness, and isolation in the more custodial schools which allow them little or no input. Fairness in disciplinary measures is important to them. Students do not desire unlimited powers. Generally, they desire to take part in rule-making and governance decisions—not in curriculum decisions and grading.

(5) Teachers have numerous opportunities to provide democratic learning experiences in the classroom and to establish a democratic climate which allows for student decision-making, but is orderly and productive. A teacher's influence is related to:

(a) Style of leadership and mode of teacher-student interaction.

(b) Types of teaching strategies employed, such as student-initiated interaction and encouragement of student expression.

(c) Types of social studies content presented, such as controversial issues.

In summary, schools, teachers, and administrators do make a difference in the democratic attitudes, skills, and knowledge which students learn. They exert multiple influences, direct and indirect, obvious and subtle.

There is a good deal of evidence to indicate that their role in the citizenship education of students is significant. Appropriate changes in formal and informal educational practices monitored by further research offer good prospects for increasing democratic education in schools and classrooms.

References

Allman-Snyder, A., et al. Classroom structure and children's perceptions of authority: An open and closed case. *Urban Education,* 1975, *10,* 131–149.

Barker, R., and Gump, P. *Big school, small school.* Stanford, CA: Stanford University Press, 1965.

Boesel, D., *Violent schools—safe schools: The safe school study report to Congress.* National Institute of Education, U.S. Government Printing Office, 1978.

Burback, H. An empirical study of powerlessness among high school students. *High School Journal,* 1972, *55,* 353–354.

DeVries, D., and Slavin, R. Teams-games-tournaments (TGT): Review of ten classroom experiments. *Journal of Research and Development in Education,* 1978, *12,* 28–38.

Dillon, S., and Grout, J. Schools and alienation. *Elementary School Journal,* 1976, *8,* 481–489.

Dozier, M. *The relative effectiveness of vicarious and experimental techniques on the development of moral judgment with groups of desegregated sixth-grade pupils.* Unpublished doctoral dissertation, University of Miami, 1974.

Ehman, L. An analysis of the relationships of selected educational variables with the political socialization of high school students. *American Educational Research Journal,* 1969, *6,* 559–580.

Ehman, L. Social studies instructional factors causing change in high school students socio-political attitudes over a two-year period. Paper presented at the annual meeting of the American Educational Research Association, New York, April, 1977.

Ehman, L. The American school in the political socialization process. *Review of Educational Research,* 1980, *50,* 99–119.

Ehman, L., and Gillespie, J. *The school as a political system.* Final report to the National Institute of Education, Project No. 3-3067, September, 1975.

Fowlkes, D. Classroom climate and political socialization. Paper presented at the annual meeting of the American Political Science Association, Chicago, September, 1976.

Godward, T. *Role and role conflicts: A study of New York State's social studies teachers as teachers and citizens.* Unpublished doctoral dissertation, Syracuse University, 1963.

Goldenson, D. An alternative view about the role of the secondary school in political socialization. *Theory and Research in Social Education,* 1978, *6,* 44–72.

Greenstein, F. *Children and politics.* New Haven, CT: Yale University Press, 1965.

Halpin, A., and Croft, D. *The organizational climate of schools.* Chicago: University of Chicago, 1963.

Hawley, W. Reforming the civics curriculum through restructuring of teacher behavior. Paper presented at the annual meeting of Midwestern Political Science Association, Chicago, 1977.

Hepburn, M. *The political involvement of social studies teachers.* Unpublished doctoral dissertation, Florida State University, 1969.

Hepburn, M. How do we know what they know? Testing the impact of the school curriculum on the political knowledge of students. *Teaching Political Science* 1980, 7(4), 425–438.

Hepburn, M., and Napier, J. Evaluation of a locally developed social studies curriculum project: Improving Citizenship Education. Paper presented at the annual meeting of the American Educational Research Association, New York, 1982.

Hepburn, M., and Napier, J. Patterns of student attitudes toward political institutions and political participation. *Teaching Political Science,* Winter 1982–83, *10,* 77–88.

Hess, R., and Torney, J. *The development of political attitudes in children.* Chicago: Aldine Publishing Co., 1967.

Jaros, D., and Canon, B. Transmitting basic political values: The role of the educational system. *The School Review,* 1969, 77, 94–107.

Johnson, D.W. Student-student interaction: The neglected variable in education. *Educational Researcher,* 1969, *10* (1), 5–10.

Jones, R.S. "Evaluating student involvement as a technique for improving citizenship education." *Theory and Research in Social Education,* December, 1975, *3,* 73–78.

Kleinert, E. Effects of high school size on student activity participation. *NASSP Bulletin,* 1969, *53,* 34–36.

Langton, K., and Jennings, M. Political socialization and the high school civics curriculum. *American Political Science Review,* 1968, *62,* 852–867.

Lewin, K. Experiments on autocratic and democratic atmospheres. *Social Frontiers,* 1938, *4,* 316–319.

Lewin, K., Lippett, R., and White, R. Patterns of aggressive behavior in experimentally created social climates. *Journal of Social Psychology,* 1939, *10,* 271-299.

Lockwood, A.L. Stage of moral development and students' reasoning on public policy issues. *Journal of Moral Education,* 1975, *5,* 51–61.

Lockwood, A.L. The effects of values clarification and moral development curricula on school-age subjects. A critical review of recent research. *Review of Educational Research,* 1978, *48,* 325–364.

Long, S., and Long, R. Controversy in the classroom: Student viewpoint and educational outcome. *Teaching Political Science,* 1975, *2,* 275–299.

Merelman, R.M. *Political socialization and educational climates: A study of two school districts.* New York: Holt, Rinehart and Winston, 1971.

Metzger, D., and Barr, R. The impact of school political systems on student political attitudes. *Theory and Research in Social Education,* 1978, *6,* 48–79.

Mosher, R.L. (ed.). *Moral education: A first generation of research and development.* New York: Praeger, 1980.

Mullis, I. Effects of home and school on learning mathematics, political knowledge and political attitudes. *National Assessment of Educational Progress,* April 1979. (Abstracted from Mullis, I., *Effects of home and school on learning mathematics and political knowledge and attitudes.* Unpublished doctoral dissertation, University of Colorado, 1978.)

O'Neill, J. The effects of a teams-games-tournaments reward structure on the self-esteem and academic achievement of ninth grade social studies students. Unpublished doctoral dissertation, University of Georgia, 1980.

Ponder, G.A., and Button, C. Student classroom initiation and political attitudes. *Contemporary Education,* 1975, *46,* 221–228.

Powell, F. Source credibility and behavioral compliance as determiners of attitude change. *Journal of Personality and Social Psychology,* 1965, *2,* 669–676.

Rafeledes, M., and Hoy, W. Student sense of alienation and pupil control orientations of high schools. *High School Journal,* 1971, *55,* 101–111.

Remy, R. High school seniors' attitudes toward their civics and government instruction. *Social Education,* 1972, *36,* 590–597.

Richards, A., and DeCecco, J. A study of student perceptions of civic education. *Journal of Social Issues,* 1975, *31,* 111–122.

Rundle, L. C. Moral development in the fifth grade classroom. Unpublished doctoral dissertation. Boston University, 1977.

Serow, R., and Strike, K. Students' attitudes toward high school governance: Implications for social education. *Theory and Research in Social Education,* 1978, *6,* 12–26.

Slavin, R. Cooperative learning. *Review of Educational Research,* 1980, *50,* 315–342.

Stentz, M., and Lambert, H. An empirical reformulation of political efficacy. *Theory and Research in Social Education,* 1977, *5,* 61–85.

Torney, J. Contemporary political socialization in elementary school and beyond. *High School Journal,* 1970, *54,* 153–163.

Torney, J., Oppenheim, A., and Farnen, R. *Civic education in ten countries.* New York: John Wiley and Sons, 1975.

Ungs, T. Attitudes toward classroom activism. *Social Science Quarterly,* 1968, *49,* 296–304.

Wasserman, E. "An alternative high school based on Kohlberg's just community approach to education." In *Moral education: A first generation of research and development,* edited by R. L. Mosher. New York: Praeger, 1980.

Wasserman, E. and Garrod, A. Application of Kohlberg's theory to curriculum and democratic schools. *Journal of British Education,* in press. 1983.

White, R., and Lippett, R. *Autocracy and democracy: An experimental inquiry.* New York: Harper and Row, 1960.

Wittes, S. School organization and political socialization. In *Political youth, traditional schools,* edited by B. Massialas. Englewood Cliffs, NJ: Prentice-Hall, 1972.

Zeigler, H. *The political world of the high school teacher.* Eugene, OR: Center for the Advanced Study of Educational Administration, University of Oregon Press, 1966.

Ziblatt, D. High school extracurricular activities and political socialization. in *Learning about politics: Reader in political socialization,* edited by R. Sigel. New York: Random House, 1970, 363–374.

The staff must be willing to take the students seriously, and when student committees have made decisions . . . to accept them.

CHAPTER THREE

Responsibility and Freedom:
It Works in Our School

Zada Koblas

Schools with democratic learning environments do exist. Seven examples are described in this chapter. In some instances, the whole school is organized so that a wide range of educational decisions will be made with student and staff participation. In other schools, the democratic learning experiences for students are provided in one area of school life only, such as involvement in setting and enforcing rules for student conduct. Sometimes a single teacher in a traditional and largely authoritarian school has provided a democratic climate for students for at least part of the student day.

The examples provided in this chapter have been chosen to represent a variety of school settings and a number of different approaches to the establishment of a democratic learning environment for the student. Examples are drawn from elementary and secondary schools, from inner-city schools in a relatively large city, and from smaller city and suburban schools. All are public schools. The initial efforts to establish a democratic climate were made in some cases by individual teachers, and in others, by parents. At least one — Project PATCH — grew out of existing curriculum. (See page 38.)

I have visited most of the schools described and talked with administrators, teachers, and, when possible, students. I learned about Project PATCH, however, at a national convention workshop, where the project was presented by the director, two students, and several members of the school staff. This chapter is written in the hope that the reader can identify with one setting or approach or another and find encouragement to act.

Parker High School: An Experiment in
Representative Democracy

A visitor to George S. Parker Senior High School in Janesville, Wisconsin, finds a large, rambling brick building set on an attractive campus at the west edge of town. Parker is one of two high schools in Janesville, a city of nearly 50,000. About half of the students in the high school of 1,700 are sons and daughters of blue-collar workers for General Motors, the city's largest employer.

School pride is reflected in the photographs, newspaper reprints, and trophies displayed in the front hall. There are many awards to the band, announcements that Parker has in recent years won the Wisconsin state basketball and baseball championships, a good citizenship award, and a commendation to Parker High School students from the city manager for the pride they exhibit in their city, school, and themselves. Newspaper articles about Unity Day, a community event involving Parker students, are also displayed.

Parker High School opened in 1967, a traditional high school with a traditional student council concerned with raising money and organizing social events—"with raising popularity," the principal said. In 1971, Parker moved to modular scheduling. During the next few years, the student council officers and their advisor, political science teacher John Eyster, became actively involved with the Wisconsin Association of Student Councils. The idea for a representative student-staff congress began to develop, with the enthusiastic support of the principal, Hugh Horswill. After a full year of study, including visits to several high schools where democratic systems were in operation, the Parker High School Congress Constitution was written and adopted in 1975. The stated purpose of the Congress is to promote the involvement of every segment of the Parker High School Community in the discussion of matters affecting the total high school community and the decisions made about them. The first Parker Congress had 25 members: 12 students (4 sophomores, 4 juniors, and 4 seniors) who were elected at large, ten members who were teachers or paraprofessionals, one member of the custodial staff, and the administrative assistant to the principal, who was a permanent member. The principal appointed a parent representative. Each person had one vote. Congress members were elected for a one-year term, except that one of the elected teacher members served as executive secretary and that person served two years to provide continuity.

The Congress drew up guidelines for the school community, and Principal Horswill's introduction included these words:

> It is our hope that we can establish an atmosphere of mutual respect, place a premium on communication, approach life at school with a positive attitude, and provide students and staff with the freedom to learn. What we do this year can and will have a lasting effect on many people in the future. Talk with each other, listen to each other, trust each other. . . . (Parker Guidelines, 1971)

At first there was open campus for everyone and a lot of unstructured time. Because some students found it difficult to make good use of their time at school, the Congress eventually decided to make open campus an earned privilege. The modified Guidelines now read in part:

INCREASED RESPONSIBILITY
Second-semester sophomores, juniors, and seniors may qualify for the advantages, opportunities, and *privileges* of Open Campus if the following four criteria are met:
1. Grade achievement—"C" average with no "F" grade.
2. Regular attendance in classes, advisory group, and study hall. No unexcused absences.
3. Citizenship—Adherence to the Parker Guidelines published in this folder.
4. Parental permission for "Open Campus." (Parker Guidelines, 1978).

Those without IR cards (open campus privilege) must be in study hall or with a signed pass in the library, open instructional labs, and resources centers. The cafeteria and commons are still free traffic areas open for the convenience of those who have earned the privilege of free movement.

The Congress is scheduled to meet during the school day once a week. On occasion, speakers such as members of the Janesville City Council have provided Congress members with background information on legislative processes. The Congress conducts some business through committees. Internal Communications, Public Relations, and Discipline are three such committees. The Educational Committee is concerned with special assemblies, enrichment programs, and curriculum matters. A student member of the Congress sits as a non-voting member of the School Board, as does a student from Janesville's other high school. Students' views are often solicited by board members at meetings. In turn, the concerns of the School Board are reported to the Parker Congress.

The Congress is allotted an operating fund from the school budget, as the principal does not think students' time is best spent raising money for routine expenditures. There have been changes in the election procedure since the inception of the program. Originally, the 12 student representatives were elected at large. Parker is a large school, and many of the student voters knew only a few of the candidates. After long discussion, the system was modified so that one representative was elected from each of the 75 home rooms. In this way, students could be represented by someone they saw every day, and there would be better communication between the students and the Congress. This modification changed the size of the Congress from the original 25 to 88. Some feel it also resulted in the election of some students with less commitment than that shown by the members of the smaller group. Originally, the student-to-staff ratio was 1:1, now it became nearly 6:1.

The number of teacher representatives in the Congress has fluctuated. At one time, teacher representation was twelve, but it has been as low as three. It was intended that faculty and staff members of the Congress would not be assigned other duties during the hour when the Congress meets. Scheduling has sometimes been a problem, and in some instances, teachers who work with students in other student activities find that these interests compete with their interest in the Congress.

Perhaps because few of the issues before the Congress concern them, the interest of the custodial and kitchen staff has dwindled over time. Currently, there is no representation from that part of the school community.

One of the issues to come before the Congress was smoking on the campus. The school administration had originally designated the parking lot behind the school as an area where smoking would be allowed. The parking lot was adjacent to the physical education area, and conflict developed between the smokers and the physical education students. Complaints from the smokers began coming to the principal's office. The matter was referred to the Congress, which, after deliberation, proposed to abolish smoking on the high school campus for everyone, including adults.

The smokers protested to Mr. Reis, the administrative assistant, who was himself opposed to the proposal. He called a meeting of all who used the smoking area. The group drew up rules for responsible smoking which included prohibitions on littering and tardiness to class. Mr. Reis requested time on the agenda of the next Congress meeting for smokers to speak. After hearing the smokers' proposal, the Congress decided on a compromise. The area behind the school has been kept open for smoking, but students can smoke there only before school and during the noon hour. Adults can smoke in the faculty lounge only.

The Congress has not spent all its time and effort on internal issues. Recently, it organized a sale of buttons to send one of the school's blind students to Holland for the Olympics for the Blind.

The administration and teachers strongly support activities which encourage students' interest in community service and world affairs. For example, the Parker Congress organized and promoted Unity Day in Janesville. On December 7, 1979, Janesville citizens joined Parker students in a four-and-one-half mile march as a response to the holding of U.S. hostages in Iran. The event was covered by local newspapers and made national television news.

Like many other school systems, Janesville schools have experienced declining enrollment and budget restrictions in recent years. Parker High School lost the services of the lay persons necessary for the modular program. Allocation of teachers to a school is now based on the number of structured classroom hours scheduled. The community called for a stricter accountability for student time. It was no longer possible to operate Parker on a modular schedule with unstructured time for students and staff. As of fall, 1980, Parker High School returned to the traditional seven-hour school day. Although the Parker Congress opposed the change, it had no power over the larger matters of resource allocation in the school system.

Hugh Horswill, the principal who sponsored the founding of the Congress, retired in 1979. His successor is William Reis, a long-time member of the faculty at Parker. The move from modular scheduling to the more structured traditional school setting made scheduling the weekly Congress meetings more difficult. The continuing success of the Parker Congress depends heavily upon the commitment of the administration to encourage meaningful involvement of the student body as well as the faculty and staff in making important decisions that affect the whole school community.

St. Paul Open School

A school should resemble a miniature democratic society. . . . The Open School's problems are examined by all affected and decisions are reached through careful study, discussion, and negotiation.[1]

The Open School in St. Paul, Minnesota, got its start in 1971 when a group of parents organized to ask the St. Paul School Board to provide a more flexible, alternative school for their children. The School Board approved the concept of an open school, but had no money to put one into operation. The parents were able to raise $200,000 through Title III of the Elementary and Secondary Education Act and from a private foundation. The alternative school opened as part of the St. Paul Public School System in a renovated warehouse building. When the school board closed one of the city's old high schools near the central business district in 1976, the Open School moved into that building. In the fall of 1979, the school moved into a newer building in a residential neighborhood.

The school is not large. There are about 400 students organized into three age groups: the early learning center (ages 5–10), the middle group (10–14), and the older age group (14–18). Each age group is served by a team of teachers. Each student selects an advisor to help design the student's program and to serve as a link with home. Students set goals for themselves and build a file of their work, which the advisor keeps. Each student is expected to become involved in the school's program and to serve the school in some way. Older students are expected to find ways to serve the community. Parents are strongly encouraged to become involved in the child's education and to do some sort of volunteer work for the school.

School Governance

Joan Sorenson was the principal when I visited the school in 1980. (Dr. Kenneth Osvold has been the principal since 1981.) She explained that the

---

[1]The quotation is from a St. Paul Open School booklet. There are descriptive articles about the school in *American Education*, October, 1978; and *Learning Magazine*, January, 1975 and March, 1977.

school is run by an Advisory Council and many committees. Some are ad hoc, some permanent. There are many meetings which bring together students, staff, and parents.

The principal is a member of the Advisory Council, which has 21 members. Ten are students, four are staff members, and six are parents or citizens-at-large. This is the policy-making body. It decides what committees are needed. Among the 19 committees active in the fall of 1980 were a Curriculum Committee and an Intercultural Committee, which heard requests for funds and made the decisions about how the school's money was spent. Parents serve on all committees. The principal has veto power as required by law. Ms. Sorenson did not remember that it had ever been used.

Curriculum

The curriculum is organized on a learning center concept. When a curriculum concern arises, a quick planning meeting called a *charette* is convened. A *charette* is similar to a brainstorming session. It meets only once, for the purpose of generating as many ideas as possible about the topic of concern. There might be, for example, a *charette* for science, for early learning, or for social studies. The ideas suggested are given to the appropriate committee for consideration.

Periodically, each team of teachers makes a schedule of classes to be offered, with a description of the content of each course and the ages for which it is intended. Students may choose to go to class or not, as they like. If a course does not attract a sufficient number of students (usually ten), the course is dropped. An exception is Advisory Skill Building Time, in which mathematics and language arts are taught at different ability and interest levels. All middle and older age students are required to attend this class daily for an hour and a half. In one listing, 17 other classes were offered to this age group: Applied Algebra, Stage Group, Bass and Guitar, Individual Music Project, Green Things, Peoples Group (ages 8–11), Mexican History and Culture, German I, Sports Heroes, Volleyball, Life Science, Peoples Group (for ages 11–18), Swimming, Protect Your Rights and Money, Open Gym, Spice and Herb Cookery, and Aerospace. Most were offered two or three days a week.

The St. Paul school system has an open enrollment policy. Any student who wishes to take a course not offered in the home building may enroll in that course wherever it is offered. The student usually arranges his or her own transportation. Many St. Paul Open School students take courses in other schools. The school provides a shuttle bus service if enough students are going to a particular destination.

Much of the students' learning is done outside the school building. For example, groups of Open School students have travelled through the United States, to Mexico, or to Europe, studying history, art, languages, and cultures. Students plan the trips themselves and raise the money for their transportation and other expenses. Older students in a consumer awareness class solve real-life consumer problems for community people. They use a nearby university law library, present findings to the city council, and work with community agencies. The principal says that about 50 percent of the older students may be out of the building at any one time.

The school's internship program provides additional community learning experiences. This unpaid work is usually scheduled during the school day for students who are 11 or older. One hundred and thirty students had internships during the 1977–78 school year. They have worked in advocacy programs such as Migrants in Action, in art centers, government offices, health clinics, small businesses, radio stations, and the local opera company.

Preparing for Graduation

Students in the Open School learn to assume a great deal of responsibility for their own education. The graduation process illustrates this well. The school's graduation requirements are based on six categories of competence: career education, community involvement and current issues, consumer awareness, cultural awareness, information findings, and personal and interpersonal skills.

To graduate, a student must demonstrate strong competency in at least three categories and some degree of competency in the others. In preparation for graduation, sophomores make a preliminary plan for demonstrating their competence as seniors. They take a diagnostic mathematics test. They list classes, activities, projects, and other learning experiences which they intend to have validated by their senior year, as well as the names of the validators. Each tenth-grade student serves as an observer on the graduation committee of a senior, so that the sophomore may become aware of the level of competence required for graduation.

Eleventh graders are expected to demonstrate math competency and one other by the end of the year. Each eleventh grader selects a five-member graduation committee and is responsible for arranging all necessary meetings of the committee. The committee includes the counselor, the school's program coordinator, the advisor, a tenth grader; and one person of the student's choice. By December, a graduation plan must be presented to the committee and parent(s). There is a required workshop for eleventh graders on preparing the graduation packet.

Seniors finalize graduation plans by December. The graduation committee provides support and ideas to the student as needed. In May, the graduation packet must be ready, and the student meets with the committee. Four of the five must recommend the student for graduation. According to students interviewed, Open School seniors feel that theirs is the hardest school in the city from which to graduate.

Project PATCH

Project PATCH (Probationary Adjustment Through Community Help) is a law-related education program developed under Title IVC in the Northport-East Northport Union Free School District in Northport, New York. It features an ombudsperson to resolve student grievances and an in-house student court providing the school with alternatives to suspension. The project director is Thomas O'Donnell.

The project began in 1969, when one social studies teacher offered a ten-week survey of the American legal system to a class as part of a Problems of Democracy elective. Now, seven different law courses are offered at Northport, and the current enrollment in these classes is 700 high school students. In addition, there is a ten-week unit on family law in the junior high taught as part of the required eighth-grade course in U.S. history and a series of units for K–6 students on jury duty and voter registration. All of these units and courses make use of realistic activities centered whenever possible on the school's operation.

Two of the high school courses are designed to fulfill course requirements in world or American history. Students learn about world cultures by studying the development of law from ancient to modern times and by comparing the laws and justice systems of representative western and non-western cultures. They study American history by focusing on major landmark constitutional decisions.

The project features "action learning." Based on knowledge from the high school legal courses, students and staff have developed model activities in a variety of areas: a student Bar Association; student advocacy programs in rights, responsibilities and consumerism; a voter registration process, K–12; jury duty, K–12; a student-operated, in-house court; a student law journal; a legal referral and research hotline; vandalism community service; a legal speakers bureau; and a moot civil court contest. Traditional classrooms are converted into medieval courtrooms, family courtrooms, and contemporary civil and criminal courtrooms. Certainly, few school systems offer such comprehensive law-related education.

The extension of the original ten-week high school course to the present level of K–12 involvement in legal studies has required in-service training for teachers. During the last few years, eight different courses for teachers and interested community members have been offered as part of Project PATCH.

The Educational Ombudsperson

In the secondary school, the position of Educational Ombudsperson was created in 1976 to investigate and resolve student complaints or problems and to insure that the Constitutional rights of students are observed in the course of the school's operation. The Ombudsperson is not a lawyer, guidance counselor, psychologist, or an administrator. He or she has no authority to overrule staff decisions, but rather is a mediator who, upon invitation, deals with controversies between students, between students and staff, with questions about student rights, grievances about discipline, and complaints about school rules. To be successful, the Ombudsperson must be tactful, fair, and trusted by students and staff, and he or she must be given enough time to do the job well.

The Ombudsperson at Northport at the time of my interviews was Stuart Goldblatt, who taught two social studies classes and devoted the rest of his time to student problems. (He has been succeeded by William Streetwieser.) In five years, Stuart handled over 400 cases. One involved a young man whose newly painted, customized Camaro was banged by a school gate as he was leaving the parking lot. He thought the school should pay for repairs. Administrators responded that the school wasn't responsible and he should have been in class at the time he was driving his car out of the lot. Stuart investigated. He found it difficult to pin down the school's insurance department, but persistence paid off. It took a notarized statement from a witness, written repair estimates, and six weeks, but the student received a check to cover the repairs.

On another occasion, a student reported that her jacket, stolen from the school cafeteria a week earlier, was being worn by another student who insisted it was his and offered to bring a sales receipt to prove it. The case was referred to Stuart by the assistant principal. Stuart took the receipt to the store, where the manager informed him that jackets such as the one in question had never been carried by the store. The young man returned the jacket. Stuart was allowed by the assistant principal to work out a resolution of the matter as an alternative to suspension for the guilty student. Stuart had a long talk with the student and was able to arrange a meeting between him and the jacket's owner. The young man apologized sincerely and offered to have the jacket dry-cleaned. Stuart considered this a positive step toward better human relations, which was preferable to a punitive exclusion from school.

When a student at Northport faces suspension, he or she may choose to confer with the Ombudsperson before disciplinary action is carried out, unless the health or safety of others is threatened. If, after investigation, the Ombudsperson feels that the student has broken a school rule, he so informs the administrator and can suggest a suitable penalty. If the case seems to be in dispute, the Ombudsperson will often refer it to the Student In-House Court, which was established to help find constructive alternatives to suspension.

The In-House Court

The In-House Court is controlled and operated by Northport student members of law classes who have passed a rigorous bar examination. All the adversary processes of the public judicial system are in operation: arraignment, preliminary hearing, jury selection, trial, and sentencing. Jurors are chosen from the school voter registration list and include students from the seventh through the twelfth grade. The presiding judge of the student In-House Court accepts the case and assigns a trial by judge, one head counsel and one assistant counsel for both prosecutor and defense, a bailiff, a court reporter, and a jury commissioner. A week is allowed for the case to be prepared. Formal proceedings are followed. If the defendant is found guilty, the judge will pronounce sentence within two days. Sentences consist of appropriate "pay back" penalties measured in units of one to fifty hours and designed to effect a positive change in the attitude and behavior of the defendant. A post-sentencing conference is held to be sure that the defendant understands the sentence clearly, and after the defendant has served the sentence, an evaluative follow-up conference is held.

By direct participation, the Northport-East Northport students are learning about justice and democratic decision-making. Project PATCH has been reviewed and state-validated and is now available to school districts for replication of all or part of the program.[2]

Children As Tutors: A Cross-Age Learning Program

Harrison Open School is a small, inner-city elementary school, which is part of the Minneapolis School System. The school is eligible for Title I services. In Minneapolis, this means that at least 26.5 percent of the students come from homes receiving assistance from Aid to Families with Dependent Children. In the fall of 1978 when Martha Steinberg Waibel's cross-age tutoring program was initiated, Harrison had 228 students, of whom 52 percent, or 120, were at least one year below grade level in mathematics or reading understanding and skills qualifying for Title I services. Martha is a Title I math resource teacher at Harrison.

Poor academic skills seemed to be breeding poor self-images in students and defensive attitudes toward classmates and teachers. Older students were harassing younger ones. In response to faculty concern, the Title I staff adopted objectives for the 1978–79 school year, which included promoting a more positive self-image among Title I students and improving relationships and communication between older and younger students, between students of different races, and between different economic groups throughout the school. To meet these objectives, the very successful Cross-

---

[2]More information about Project PATCH is available from the Director, Thomas O'Donnell, Northport-East Northport Union Free School District, Northport, NY 11768.

Age Tutoring Program was developed.

Cross-age tutoring means that older children help younger children to learn. The team of Title I teachers had a two-part task: (1) to provide a cadre of tutors prepared to tutor someone with less ability, and (2) to work out some acceptable means of delivering the service. It required a recruitment program, communication with parents, and a tutor-training program.

Other teachers were involved from the beginning. The program was explained at faculty meetings, and teachers were asked (1) to encourage students to apply for tutoring positions, (2) to sign student application forms, and (3) to list Title I students who might benefit from the tutoring. Teachers were asked to choose the days of the week and the time of day when students from their classes might be tutored.

Applications forms for older students who might want to tutor were distributed throughout the school. Fifteen students applied. The program was explained and each student, in signing the application form, committed himself or herself to a six-week training class and three 20-minute tutoring sessions per week with a student who needed help. Tutors would be trained to give this assistance by Martha and an aide.

A letter explaining the program and the commitment made by the child was sent to parents, who were asked to sign a permission form. Then the tutor training sessions began. These lasted about six weeks and were held at a time of day called Option Time at Harrison, when students choose a class from a wide range of electives. The tutoring class faced some serious competition from electives such as volleyball and pottery making.

To begin the training, tutors were given exercises and activities to promote their own understanding of the concept to be taught. Each tutor had to demonstrate an understanding of the concept before he or she was considered qualified to teach it. After completing an exercise, the tutors discussed it, developing a step-by-step description of it and assigning an appropriate time to each of its parts. The lesson was then rehearsed with another tutor. Again, the tutors met together to clear up any problems with the lesson. Each made a copy of the lesson plan for use with his or her pupil. Later, the tutors developed a general lesson plan that could be used with any concept lesson.

The tutors were given instruction in observing student progress, respecting the student's right to privacy, and keeping student attention. Tutors were shown how to encourage their students to feel that they can succeed, to try again when discouraged, and to believe that it is not too hard after all. Tutors also learned to "positrate"—that is, to concentrate on the positive characteristics of another person, and to communicate in words an awareness of these positive features.

Anyone in the Title I program who wants to tutor someone with less ability can sign up for tutor training at Harrison. Tutors do not have to be the top students in their age groups. Those who have mastered a math skill can find someone younger to work with. Sometimes bright, quick younger students tutor older ones.

By the end of the year, math scores on the school's standardized tests improved significantly for both the tutors and the tutored, but perhaps the greatest successes of the tutoring program were the increased caring and sharing, cooperative behavior, concerned *cross-cultural* interaction, and the improved self-confidence evident in those who learned to teach something valuable to another.[3]

Consumer Action Service:
A Student-Operated Community Service

Joe Nathan was impressed by his students' enthusiasm and willingness to work. His class in ecology had recently been successful with a project to eliminate a heavy stench in the industrial neighborhood surrounding their school building in St. Paul. It had been hard work. Students had talked with public interest groups, researched odor pollution standards, consulted lawyers, written complaints, and testified at a hearing. The Pollution Control Agency had found four industrial plants in violation of the pollution ordinances and order compliance.

Now his class of 12- to 17-year-olds at the St. Paul Open School was studying consumer concerns. The course was entitled "Protect Your Rights and Money." Joe suggested to students that they might operate a service for consumers if they dealt only with small local cases. The students would improve their skills, get practical experience, and provide some service to the community. The students agreed enthusiastically, and the Consumer Action Service was launched.

Obtaining Cases and Establishing Procedures

To obtain cases, students wrote a one-page leaflet explaining their services, listing previous successes and the names of some of the agencies they had worked with, and stating the limits of the student service. A local quick-print shop agreed to donate the printing. The leaflets were distributed in libraries, stores, and neighborhood shopping centers. Class members wrote short articles for neighborhood newspapers. City newspapers and television stations carried stories about the project. A bank donated a booth in the downtown areas where the students distributed leaflets and received complaints for later action.

Each case began as a project for the whole class. Students first defined clearly what the problem was. They decided what information they needed

---

[3]A 20-page explanation of the program, entitled *Children as Tutors,* is available for $5.00 from Martha Waibel, 2617 East 24th St., Minneapolis, MN 55406.

and assigned a class member to get it. Joe took part in the discussion, asking questions, and guiding students to be more specific. When it was time to plan further action, Joe listed student suggestions on the chalkboard. The merits of each suggestion were discussed. One strategy was chosen and volunteers enrolled. Students discussed with Joe exactly what steps were necessary to perform the task. Joe checked the letters they wrote. The students role-played their telephone calls, and Joe monitored these tele-phoning skills until he was sure they could work alone. Whenever any action was taken, a follow-up report was made, and the class decided how to proceed. Sometimes it was necessary to change tactics. Students checked with government agencies, law libraries, and sometimes with lawyers. They wrote letters, interviewed people, and spoke before community com-mittees. After a case was closed, the class reviewed it, determining what they had learned and suggesting ways to improve their procedures.

Students in Action

Among the cases, which the Consumer Action Service (CAS) handled were these: A man had purchased an insurance policy on his two daughters. His widow made premium payments on the policy for several years after he died and then discovered that the policy contained a clause stating that if her husband died the policy would be paid up. The insurance company refused to refund the premiums paid since the man's death. CAS helped her to collect.

A woman who lived in a federally subsidized housing project incurred damage to her personal belongings when a water pipe in her apartment broke. She was unsuccessful in collecting damages until the class took the case. This was one of their most difficult cases because of the amount of persistence needed to get a response from several government agencies and because of the difficulty of locating someone who had authority to act.

A family bought a van and was promised that a radio would be installed in it. The dealer's radio stock was temporarily depleted. After several weeks, the family began calling the dealer but got no radio. CAS helped and within a week the radio had been installed.

Joe and a colleague have eight suggestions for setting up a consumer action service in a social studies class.[4] In condensed form they are:

1. Think about your role as a teacher. You are the organizer and stimu-lator. Make reading material available to help students learn about the rights and responsibilities of consumers. Arrange for guest speakers. See that adequate planning, practice, and review are done for each case.

2. Before looking for cases, develop students' interest in the subject and encourage them to believe that they can help people with consumer problems.

---

[4]A full description of this learning activity and seven suggestions for conducting it can be found in K. Branan and J. Nathan, "Being Ripped Off? Call A Kid," *Learning Magazine*, March 1977, 76–86.

3. Visit or bring in people from radio, television, or newspaper consumer services and from local and state consumer protection agencies and the Better Busines Bureau. Try to visit a small claims court.

4. Help students to prepare a simple brochure to explain their services. Ask people to contact you by mail only.

5. Make a list of the skills that you want students to develop and spend class time teaching them.

6. Work out a clear framework for problem solving. State the problem as seen by the complainant, by the person against whom the complaint is being made, and by the class. If these three statements are different, go over the differences with the person who is bringing the complaint. List possible strategies. Discuss their strengths and weaknesses and decide on one. Then be sure that the volunteers who will work on the case know exactly what to do and practice the necessary skills. Conduct a follow-up discussion whenever any action has been taken. Change the strategy when necessary.

7. Develop a good system of forms and filing that the students themselves can understand and use. Joe felt that Consumer Action Service accomplished several things which were important for young people. They learn how important it is to read carefully. Working with contracts and other ordinary legal papers demonstrated this clearly.

8. Communicate to the community that the class is not designed to teach negative attitudes toward government or business, but aims instead to teach *both rights and responsibilities.* Good programs have been ruined because this purpose was not understood.

Consumer Action Service gave students an opportunity on a day-to-day basis to be involved in improving society. They were learning to join with others in serving their community. Making careful decisions, finding appropriate information, and using community services were all part of the work of CAS. These young people not only grew intellectually, but they learned democratic life skills which should help them to assume responsibility and to participate effectively in their society.

The Cluster School

In 1974 an alternative high school based on Kohlberg's concept of the "just community" was set up in Cambridge, Massachusetts. The purpose was to create conditions for moral growth through a curriculum featuring discussion of moral issues and through a governing structure based on participatory democracy.[5]

---

[5]This account is based on correspondence with and articles by Elsa Wasserman, a counselor in the Cambridge Public Schools and a member of the staff of the Cluster School. See her article in *Social Education,* April 1976, pp. 203–207. See also *The development of an alternative high school based on Kohlberg's just community approach to education.* Unpublished Ed.D. dissertation, Boston University School of Education, 1977.

Students, Staff, and Program

The Cluster School was established as an alternative school within Cambridge High and Latin School, a large urban high school. The staff is made up of regular Cambridge High School teachers who volunteered to be part of the program. In 1976 there were seven staff members, three of whom taught part of the day in the regular high school. The students also were volunteers who in the first years were chosen by lot from the list of those wanting to enroll. In 1976 there was a total of 72 students in the four high school grades of the alternative school.

All of the students take a core of English and social studies courses which center on moral discussions and role-playing activities and which examine the relationship of the governing structure of the school to that of the broader society. Other courses are also offered in the Cluster School, and the students are free to take classes in the regular comprehensive Cambridge High and Latin School. They also participate in any extracurricular activities which the high school offers. They are not cut off, therefore, from the regular student body, as is the case in many alternative schools, especially those in a separate building.

The Community Meeting

The Cluster School has its own governing body, makes its own rules, and handles its own disciplinary problems. The community meeting is the central institution of government. No major decisions are made without consulting the broader community. It is in these meetings that rules and policies are set for the school, including rules about disruptive behavior, vandalism, cutting classes, use of drugs, theft, and grading. Each staff member and each student has one vote in a community meeting.

Procedures to ensure that these meetings will run smoothly have developed over time. For instance, at first, staff members chaired the meetings, but later, students took over. Each meeting's agenda is circulated in advance, and all issues are discussed in small groups of not more than 12 before the meeting takes place. In this way, students are more personally involved in the discussions, issues are clarified, role-taking and exposure to higher-stage reasoning is encouraged, and a sense of community is developed. A straw vote is often taken in the community meeting as a means of determining when to close discussion. When there seems to be substantial agreement about an issue, a binding vote is taken, and the result determines policy or rule for the community.

Committees

While the community meetings are concerned with matters affecting the whole community, advisor groups help students with personal or academic problems. These are small support groups which are often able to help a student clarify a problem and suggest ideas for the solution.

A Discipline Committee decides how to treat staff or students who break school rules. The representatives on the committee are students selected at random from each advisor group and alternated regularly. One staff member serves. Appeals can be made to the community meeting.

Relationship to Kohlberg, His Philosophy, and Research

The staff has had the guidance of Harvard's Lawrence Kohlberg and two associates. During the summer before the school opened, Kohlberg served as advisor while plans were being made for the school's organization and operation. Once the school opened, weekly evening meetings were held to review the previous community meeting and discuss other school concerns. These are open to interested students. Workshops for staff members help them to learn to lead moral discussions and integrate them into the curriculum. These staff meetings have been considered vital to the school's success.

Although many other alternative schools have failed, the Cluster School staff believes that it can succeed in maintaining its participatory democratic structure because:

(1) Participatory democracy is perceived as a central educational goal, not just one of many important, but conflicting goals.

(2) The focus is on issues of morality and fairness, rather than administrative matters which many students find uninteresting.

(3) The community is small enough so that decisions can be made in community meetings where everyone participates and issues can be discussed in small groups in preparation for the meeting.

(4) There is a firm commitment to provide both direct and indirect conditions for moral growth. By "direct conditions" Kohlberg means providing meaningful discussions and small group and community interaction. "Indirect conditions" refers to the general climate of the school.

Results

Has this school experience made a difference in the lives of the students? The staff notes a high level of morale and a sense of community in students. Students have taken responsibility for their own behavior and the behavior of others. They have developed participation skills and, in some cases, leadership skills which they can be expected to carry into their adult lives as members of the broader community. There have been changes for the better in the behavior of students who have long had difficulties in school.

There are long term benefits as well. After the Cluster School had been in operation for a few years, the Superintendent of Schools in Cambridge decided to adopt some of its practices in the large high school. The student

Students are concerned with fairness and other questions of justice.

body is too large to attempt whole community meetings as in the Cluster School, but several avenues for student/staff discussion and resolution of conflict have been found. A Fairness Committee with voluntary membership hears and resolves grievances and initiates revisions of certain school policies and rules. A Teacher/Advisor Program was begun, and a Student Service Project trains students in counseling and advocacy skills. Student Advocates listen to the problems of other students and often suggest means to help inside and outside of the school.

Fairness Committees and the just community approach have become part of the school government in numerous schools across the country, at both elementary and secondary levels. (Some examples are found in Scarsdale, New York; Bakersfield, California; and Brookline and Reading, Massachusetts.

Conclusions

In gathering material for this chapter, I have talked with teachers, principals, counselors, and consultants who have been participants in and observers of these and other efforts to increase student responsibility and involvement in their schools. I pass along to you their observations and suggestions. Parents are usually strong supporters of a well-thought-out idea for improving the school climate, and it is often a good idea to begin with a parent group. The St. Paul Open School, described in this chapter, was begun by parent initiative, and it was parents who raised the money for it. The Cluster School had strong parental involvement from the beginning.

Not much can be done without strong administrative support. Administrative *commitment* is probably a better phrase. In a school where scheduling is difficult and money is limited, it takes commitment on the part of the administration to find time in the school day for students and staff to participate in the necessary group meetings. The administrator also plays an important role in generating and maintaining staff support for the program. A strong parent group often helps bolster administrative support.

The kinds of issues that students are allowed to act upon make a difference. Only a fraction of a student body will be interested in planning a dance or the auditorium program. Students are often bored with administrative matters, such as scheduling, and want the staff to work these out. They are much more likely to be interested in policy decisions that affect the whole school. They are concerned over fairness and other questions of justice. They want a forum where their grievances can be heard and solutions can be discussed. They are interested in community service that has recognized values.

A successful program requires staff support. Even a single classroom effort like Martha Waibel's cross-age tutoring program, for example, depends upon the willingness of other teachers to release tutors and their pupils from classes. Parker High School depends on teachers' and custodial staff members' willingness to take an active part in the Congress, not just during the first year, but on a continuing basis. The staff must be willing to take the students seriously, and when student committees have made decisions, the staff must be willing to accept them. Fairness must extend beyond student organizations. Fairness must guide the responses of teachers and administrators as well. A climate of fairness is essential to democratization of schools and classrooms.

CHAPTER FOUR

Practicing What We Teach:
Promoting Democratic Experiences in
the Classroom

Ronald L. VanSickle

Five values characterize a learning situation where democracy is practiced: (1) Each student has an equal opportunity to learn. (2) The welfare of
each individual is maximized. (3) The system of rewards and penalties is
responsive to individual performance. (4) Each individual is held responsible for his or her effect on the welfare of others. (5) Knowledge, skills, and
attitudes are taught which promote each individual's welfare and the
welfare of the classroom group and larger society in such a way that they in
turn are likely to enhance each individual's welfare. Implementing these
values in the academic and nonacademic life of a classroom group is a
demanding, yet crucial task in a society which aspires to be democratic.

It is important to note from the beginning that democratic classrooms are
highly structured classrooms. Democracy does not mean freedom to do
anything one wishes. Democracy *does* mean freedom to participate in and
to influence the decision-making procedures affecting one's life. Democratic classrooms require clear-cut decision-making procedures, clearly defined limits for student participation and influence, explicit consequences
for supporting or violating democratically instituted decisions, established
procedures and roles for implementing and enforcing decisions, and
well-defined domains of personal freedom and social responsibility. Democratic classrooms will not have less structure than authoritarian classrooms. The difference is that students in democratic classrooms will have
opportunities to use the structure to realize their values and interests.

In order to explain how democratic experiences can be promoted in the
classroom, four topics will be addressed in this chapter. First, the social and
political dimensions of a classroom group will be identified. Second, ways
of making democracy operational in the classroom will be examined in
terms of student and teacher behavior. Third, thirteen recommendations

for producing democratic classroom experiences will be presented and illustrated. Fourth, cautions and guidelines will be considered.

Social and Political Dimensions of the Classroom

A classroom has social and political dimensions, including status systems, decision-making procedures, affective relationships, and social control processes.[1] Teachers and students must clearly understand these concepts in order to think and act coherently regarding democracy in the classroom. These dimensions must be molded to transmit the abstract values which characterize a democratic classroom.

Status systems are the ways in which members of a group rank each other from better to worse. The rankings are based on some generally valued characteristic or characteristics such as academic ability, athletic skill, physical appearance, ethnic background, social class, and sex. Students and teachers use these and other status characteristics to generate expectations for themselves and others, extend or withhold opportunities, and evaluate their own and others' performances. In classrooms, status systems create and destroy opportunities and incentives to learn and participate. Status systems are a fundamental part of human group life and cannot be eliminated. A classroom with a highly centralized status system will exhibit widespread agreement regarding who is ranked at the high, middle, and low levels. A few students will be consistently rated highly by many of their peers. A classroom with a diffuse status system will have relatively little agreement. Students will be inconsistently rated; many students will be rated fairly highly by at least a few others. The nature and application of the status systems can have a profound effect on the degree to which democracy is practiced in a classroom.

Decision-making procedures are the ways in which a group selects courses of action, allocates resources, assigns responsibilities, and evaluates performance. The procedures can involve many people, a few people, or varying numbers, depending on the questions to be decided. The decision-making procedures used in a classroom are obviously a major determinant of the degree of democracy in a classroom. In a highly authoritarian classroom, the teacher has control over almost all decisions. On the other hand, in a highly democratic classroom, students do not necessarily participate in all decisions, but participation is more general.

Affective relationships are the feelings of liking, respect, and inclusion which group members have for themselves and other members of the

---

[1] In order to avoid a large number of research citations, two sources are noted as good reviews of the research supporting claims made in the introductory sections of this chapter. (1) VanSickle, Ronald L., "Neutralizing Status Constraints on Student Performance in Small Group Activities," *Theory and Research in Social Education,* 7(2): 1–33, 1979. (2) Schmuck, Richard A., and Schmuck, Patricia A., *Group Processes in the Classroom,* 3rd edition, William C. Brown, 1979.

group. These feelings might not appear crucial for a society to be democratic. However, in a group the size of a classroom group, these feelings have major effects on student behavior and performance. They affect and are affected by the status systems and decision-making procedures operating in the class. Attention to students' affective relationships is a means of influencing the degree of classroom democracy.

Social control processes are the ways in which group members' behaviors are regulated to conform to socially desirable patterns. The conforming behavior is not necessarily desirable from the teacher's perspective. Even in a classroom characterized by the teacher's strong disciplinary control, some social control resides with the students. This will be clear to any teacher who has found it difficult to motivate students to do homework, participate actively in discussions, or ask questions. Sometimes, mediocre academic performance is expected, and students who "ruin the curve" receive criticism from their peers. In especially troubled classes, social control processes among the students can provoke and reward academically disruptive behavior. "Social control" has an authoritarian ring to it, but it can be a source of opportunities for democratic classroom experiences.

Democratic Behavior in the Classroom

It is important to be specific about the nature of democracy in a classroom. Thinking in terms of status systems, decision-making procedures, affective relationships, and social control will help. However, ways are needed for assessing the success of efforts to democratize a classroom. Three outcomes which can be used for this purpose are student participation rates, student influence rates, and academic performance.

Participation rates are frequencies of interpersonal communication. Initiation rate, for example, is a measure of how often a student overtly participates in the group by stating or asking something. A response rate is a measure of how often a student responds verbally or nonverbally to questions or requests. Distribution rate of performance opportunities refers to how often students are given opportunities to say or do something. Other examples of participation rates are interaction rates, attempts to influence others, and occurrences of cross-status interaction.

Student influence rates measure how often others accept a student's judgment and suggestions as valid and worth using as guides for action. The ideas of a student with considerable influence will be readily accepted in discussions and considered for implementation. An influential student does not necessarily make great efforts to be persuasive. Teachers as well as students are susceptible to student influence.

Academic performance refers to the degree to which students achieve instructional goals and objectives in light of their academic ability. Since schools exist to teach people, a democratic classroom, like any other, must be evaluated in part on how well students learn in that environment. Even though it is difficult to do, learning should be measured against students' academic potential.

Democracy in the classroom is a matter of degree; teachers and the classroom environment can be viewed on a continuum from more to less democratic. Rather than attempting to set up an ideal democratic classroom, it will be more useful for teachers to think about how to move from a less democratic position on the continuum to a more democratic one. Given that democracy is relative, it should be useful to clarify the endpoints of the continuum. The following are sketches of a highly undemocratic and a highly democratic classroom.

An Undemocratic Classroom. In the undemocratic classroom, student participation, influence, and academic performance are closely related to the social and political dimensions of classroom life. A highly centralized status system operates. Highly centralized decision-making procedures prevail. Competitive, status-oriented affective relationships exist. Centralized overtly coercive social control processes hold sway.

Student status is generally based on academic ability, as well as socially relevant characteristics (for example, ethnicity, athletic skill, social class, and sex). Students agree with a high degree of consistency regarding each individual's status. Student participation in instruction is closely related to status, with the students of higher status dominating. Given a choice, both the teacher and the students accept ideas and suggestions of higher status students more readily than those of lower status students. Academic performance is positively related to status, partly as a result of differential behavior by the teacher and the teacher's and students' status-related expectations for individuals' performances.

The teacher makes nearly all decisions regarding curriculum, instruction, student behavior, penalties, evaluation, and schedules. This highly centralized decision-making minimizes active student participation in classroom life and restricts the opportunity for students to exert influence in their school environment.

Student affective relationships are weak and neutral, except in the case of students with strong out-of-class relationships. There is a sense of individual competition among students. Students give little or no help to one another. They feel little closeness or caring for a large majority of students in the class. When cooperation, helping, and caring are exhibited, they occur almost exclusively among students of similar status. Due to the weak affective relationships, student participation and influence are low. Academic performance probably is depressed as well. Students who feel disliked in a class tend to under-achieve more often and to a greater degree than students who feel liked even if they actually are not.

Most student behavior is regulated by the teacher according to inflexible rules or personal preferences. In the latter case, enforcement of rules and administration of penalties tend to correlate with the status system. Students of lower status tend to experience more strict enforcement than those of higher status. The principal direct effects of teacher-centered social control are few opportunities for students to have constructive influence in the classroom.

A Democratic Classroom. In a highly democratic classroom, student participation, influence, and academic performance are related differently to the social and political dimensions. The status system is somewhat diffuse. Decision-making procedures involve substantial student participation. Affective relationships are cooperative and personalized. Social control is exercised by both the teacher and the students, mostly through consensual processes.

Student status is based partly on academic ability, as well as other socially relevant characteristics. However, students have opportunities to demonstrate their strengths publicly and to be recognized for them in a way which minimizes status-related expectations. Students do not agree very consistently regarding each individual's status level, because they use individual as well as social characteristics to judge one another. Student participation and influence are more widespread and equitable because of the weaker status system. In the absence of differential teacher behavior and strong status-related expectations, academic performance only weakly influences status.

Students have explicit opportunities to influence the teacher's decision-making, and, in some cases, they have the authority to make the decisions. Students recommend or choose some topics for study. Instructional activities preferred by students are used whenever possible and appropriate. Evaluation alternatives are considered, and students are involved in evaluation to some extent. A group of students serves as an advisory body to the teacher on various questions and problems facing the class. Student participation and influence in classroom life are high as a result.

Student affective relationships are relatively strong and predominately positive. There is little sense of individual competition, but a relatively strong sense of cooperation and consideration. Helping others with instructional tasks is encouraged. All, or nearly all, students feel that some others, including the teacher, care about how they are doing. Student participation and influence is reasonably equitable as a result. Academic performance is strongly and positively tied to potential, owing to the minimal alienation in the classroom.

Student behavior is regulated by the teacher according to consensually established rules and by explicit student support for the rules. Rules, their justifications, and penalties for violating them are discussed and formulated by the students in consultation with the teacher. The high degree of consensus ensures that overtly coercive enforcement seldom occurs. Student influence is high as a result of such social control processes.

Promoting Democratic Classroom Experiences

Thus far, we have examined the social and political dimensions of classroom life, the outcomes for students related to those dimensions, and the characteristics of more and less democratic classrooms in light of those dimensions and outcomes. With these ideas in mind, let us examine a set of recommendations for teachers which are likely to move the classroom toward the democratic end of the continuum.[2]

(1) *Avoid differential behavior toward students of different status and thus avoid communicating negative expectations.*

Researchers have observed repeatedly that students of lower status tend to receive less academic feedback from teachers than students of higher status. Also, teachers tend to call on higher status students much more often than lower status students. Higher status students tend to receive more rewards and receptive attention from teachers than lower status students. Teachers tend to criticize and control the behavior of lower status students considerably more than their higher status classmates.

Since these conditions are widespread, teachers who wish to democratize their classrooms should review their behavior for these negative, status-related behaviors. Simply counting the number of times each student is called on, criticized, provided academic feedback, given time to answer a question, and so forth will reveal differential behavior if it exists. Tape recording or observations by students or colleagues are useful approaches to monitoring. Once differential behavior is identified, a teacher can set objectives for more equitable treatment of students and periodically monitor his or her teaching. Eliminating differential behavior is one way of distributing participation opportunities more equitably. As a side benefit, the teacher will avoid demonstrating low expectations to lower status students and displaying them to the other students. Destructive self-

[2]Research and development supporting the recommendations can be found in the following references: (1) Brophy and Good, 1974; Good, Sikes, and Brophy, 1973; Rist, 1970; Rothbart, Dalfen, and Barrett, 1971. (2) Smith, 1981; Bossert, 1979. (3) Cohen, Lockheed, and Lohman, 1976; Cohen and Sharen, 1977. (6) Schmuck and Schmuck, 1979. (7) Beyer and Brostoff, 1979; Newmann and Oliver, 1970. (9) Simon, Howe, and Kirschenbaum, 1972. (10) Caramia and Knight, 1980. (11) Schmuck and Schmuck, 1979. (12) Aronson, Bridgeman, and Geffner, 1978; DeVries and Slavin, 1978; Slavin, 1978; Slavin, 1980. (13) Ehman, 1979; Hunt and Metcalf, 1968; Oliver and Shaver, 1966; Shaver and Larkins, 1973.

fulfilling prophecies for participation, influence, and academic performance are difficult enough to counteract without the teacher reinforcing them.

(2) *Avoid evaluation practices which reinforce the ability status system of self-fulfilling prophecies.*

When information about students' academic performances is widely known within a class, the ability status system is strongly reinforced. At least, a teacher can avoid posting grades, distributing students' papers consistently from best to worst, and commenting publicly on students who perform poorly. If a lower status student incorrectly answers a question during recitation, rephrasing the question or prompting the student can create a second opportunity for him or her to demonstrate competence (Smith, 1981). Broadcasting bad news is likely to motivate students of lower status to avoid participation, minimize their influence over other members of the class, and depress their academic performances. Students need constructive academic feedback about their errors, but it should be given privately.

Another way to avoid general knowledge of students' academic performances is to use multiple evaluation formats. If students can choose among objective, written, oral, graphic, and other ways of demonstrating their achievement, comparisons among students by their peers will be considerably more difficult. Also, student strengths can be emphasized. For example, tape-recorded oral tests can be used with students who have significant problems in reading comprehension, in order to enable them to demonstrate their achievement more validly.

(3) *Provide lower status students with opportunities to teach other students.*

One of the most effective ways to counteract expectations of low performance is to give students of lower status an opportunity to demonstrate their competence to others. It is important to remember that lower status is not synonymous with lower ability. Also, most students who have demonstrated low academic performance over a long term have competence in some areas which might be tapped. For example, a rural student with knowledge of American wildlife could present information in a history or anthropology class. A student with some art talent could show a civics class how to reproduce political cartoons. The key is to focus the class members' attention on a student of lower status at a time when he or she can demonstrate competence. Questionnaires or interviews will help a teacher collect information and clues about students' interests and skills. Participation, influence, and academic performance are likely to increase as a result of students teaching other students.

(4) *Provide public recognition for students' academic and nonacademic achievements.*

Negative expectations can be weakened and positive expectations strengthened when students' accomplishments are recognized and valued by other students. A variety of classroom performances can be recognized in playing simulation games, preparing bulletin boards or displays, and interviewing to collect data. Nonacademic school achievement can be applauded as well, including excellent performances in athletics, music, or dramatics, or outstanding contributions to school service projects and events such as bake sales, homecoming, distributive education contests, etc. School newspapers, students, and faculty can be useful sources of information. Students' contributions to community life, such as leadership in religious groups, volunteer work as candy stripers at the hospital, or scouting achievements, can also be recognized. Recognition of a variety of achievements can weaken the operating assumption that people who are not well known in school are one-dimensional in ability.

The format for recognizing student performance will vary and will depend partly on the age of the students. While younger students might be very pleased to have their teacher periodically take time to congratulate them publicly, some high school students might be embarrassed. A teacher or teachers could employ a bulletin board display or a class newsletter. Perhaps the approach with the greatest potential is to encourage students to recognize each other. A committee of students could identify achievements of various types and, with the teacher's guidance, carry out the public recognition. Recognizing student achievement in a variety of areas can break down low expectations, increase students' influence with others, enhance mutual approval and respect among students, and indirectly improve academic performance by creating a more motivating and rewarding classroom environment.

(5) *Present students with options regarding what will be taught and how it will be taught.*

Planning high quality instruction is a time-consuming activity, and involving students in the process might seem like a needless complication. However, presenting students with opportunities to make some decisions regarding classroom instruction can increase student participation, influence, and possibly academic achievement. Students could select three or four topics for study from a list of several valuable topics after a general discussion of them. Students in small groups could suggest topics for study within an area specified by the teacher. Also, students could select instructional techniques that they prefer from a set of options which the teacher believes to be appropriate and feasible, given the learning objectives and the limits of his or her time and resources. By presenting options for students, the teacher does not abdicate authority. He or she shares decision-making power with the students in a structured way which still upholds the teacher as the instructional expert with responsibility for implementing curriculum.

(6) *Form a student steering committee to assist in making decisions about classroom issues.*

Students with a great deal of influence and popularity among their peers can be appointed to a steering committee by the teacher in order to use their influence in constructive ways. The teacher would present questions which need answering to the committee, which would be charged with the reponsibility of recommending ideas and sometimes making binding decisions within clearly specified limits. Some of the questions could involve course content and instruction, student evaluation procedures, classroom procedures, evaluation of teaching, and issues concerning student behavior.

The scope and power granted the steering committee would depend on the members' initial attitudes toward school, the course, and the teacher. There is no necessity of giving broad power; students will need to learn how to make decisions effectively. The scope and authority of the steering committee can be broadened by the teacher as the innovation of a steering committee is institutionalized within the group and as students' decision-making skills increase. The composition of the committee should change occasionally. Students' participation and influence can be greatly increased by this technique and classroom status systems can be harnessed to motivate effort toward desirable academic and social goals.

(7) *Involve students in the formative evaluation of their peers' academic performances.*

Involving students in the evaluations of other students' academic performances clearly demonstrates that a teacher values students' ideas. Student influence will probably increase if students participate in a major classroom process like evaluation. The kind of evaluation that students can constructively perform is formative. Summative evaluation and the assignment of grades should generally be left to the teacher in recognition of his or her expertise. However, even in this area, student evaluations and recommendations could be considered.

Discussion and writing are two areas in which students' evaluation of peers can be a straightforward process. If the teacher attempts to teach a set of effective discussion techniques, then students can be assigned to observe and rate other students' performances in small group discussions. The resulting experience and data can be useful to both the observed and observing students. Students can read each other's writing and provide constructive feedback by identifying the main points or feelings of an essay, summarizing the essay in a single sentence, and choosing words which summarize it. If the writer does not see the evaluator's comments as appropriate, then revision is clearly needed.

(8) *Provide opportunities for students to tutor other students.*

Peer tutoring is likely to benefit the tutor as well as the tutored. Helping someone else to learn requires the tutor to organize and present previously learned knowledge coherently. In much the same way that writing improves a writer's understanding of the relationships and implications of a subject, teaching deepens a tutor's insights. The academic benefits of effective tutoring for the tutored are obvious.

In addition to the academic benefits, there are desirable social outcomes. A tutoring relationship can open communication between students of above average and below average achievement. As a result of status systems based on ability, communication between high and low achievers is usually restricted. Friendly, helpful interaction provides personal insights that can reduce the social distance between the students. A capable, but not very influential student can experience a new and higher degree of influence in a tutoring relationship. Peer tutoring will not totally dismantle a hierarchy determined by academic ability, but it can provide opportunities for students to interact constructively when there would typically be little interaction of any kind.

(9) *Interview students publicly about their views on a wide variety of academic and nonacademic topics and issues.*

Public interviews give students opportunities to catch glimpses of the way life looks to other students in the class. Interviews can range over a wide variety of topics, such as football, space exploration, television shows, politics, heroes, and friendship. A teacher can predetermine and announce what kinds of subjects are out of bounds. Since this is not a highly structured technique, the student being interviewed should have the option of not answering a question that seems too personal. The teacher should be the interviewer until students are sensitive to the ground rules and know what is going to happen.

Brief interviews with students can help to break down stereotypes based on academic ability, ethnic and class backgrounds, and sex, which students and teachers easily develop in a task-centered, large-group, academic atmosphere. Student relationships can be initiated and strengthened as a result of empathy and an awareness of shared interests and experiences. As the classroom becomes a more personalized environment and the status system becomes more diffuse, the proportion of students working up to their academic potential can rise.

(10) *Involve small groups in projects that require cooperative efforts for successful completion.*

Cooperative small group projects which need contributions from all students can help to improve affective relationships within a class. A teacher can divide the class into groups reflecting social, academic, and sexual balance. Students' expectations for each other's performances will greatly reinforce the effects of the teacher's expectations. Influence, mutual respect, and liking among students will probably be promoted by such cooperative projects. Participation by nearly all members is likely to be fairly high. Because of mutually reinforcing expectations and informal peer teaching, academic achievement is likely to be good.

For best results, the project should be multidimensional, so that conventional academic skills are not the only requirements for success. In addition to a written report, the project could involve constructing a model, making posters, presenting a play or skit, or creating a bulletin board display. The teacher's role involves locating and preparing data sources, acting as a resource person and consultant for each group, monitoring each group's progress, and assisting each group in preparing its report and presentation.

(11) *Enlist the students' help in developing guidelines for appropriate behavior.*

A key way to include students in constructive social control is to develop cooperatively a set of behavioral guidelines for the class. This strategy is not necessarily the first that a teacher would use in a course, although it could be. Students are not likely to expect involvement in disciplinary matters, and the teacher must clearly communicate that he or she is not abdicating responsibility. If students are included in setting or revising behavioral guidelines, their expectations for constructive behavior can greatly magnify a teacher's influence, because his or her authority then represents the collective will of the group.

When initiating a discussion intended to produce a set of guidelines, a teacher must clarify what can and cannot be considered. Certain school regulations are not within a teacher's authority to alter regardless of the merits of a proposed change. Also, a teacher might regard certain conditions as essential for him or her to function effectively. If the limits are clear from the beginning, students are not likely to feel that the teacher is insincere when limits must be imposed. Also, a teacher must structure the discussion and generation of guidelines so that widespread student participation is guaranteed. Less verbally assertive students are likely to support behavior that seems conventional. They can counterbalance students with more free-wheeling inclinations.

With the aid of the teacher, students should test proposals for behavioral guidelines. To what extent will a proposed guideline help or hinder them to achieve academically? To what extent will a proposed guideline enhance or reduce student participation in instructional activities? For example, a student might recommend that students not be required to raise their hands for recognition in a class discussion. It should be clear to students that in some large groups discussion will be dominated by verbally aggressive students and numerous useful contributions will not be made by less assertive students. The behavioral guidelines then can be amended to take this problem into account.

Developing guidelines for appropriate behavior provides direct opportunities for students to exercise influence over their immediate social environment. Further, the guidelines can increase student participation in classroom instruction by setting guidelines that assume and facilitate participation. Finally, involving students can help to minimize behavior problems by adding the students' influence to the teacher's when disruptive incidents occur.

(12) *Organize students into learning teams characterized by cooperative effort, group rewards, and public recognition.*

Team learning techniques have the potential to democratize a class by increasing student participation rates, influence rates, and academic performance. Three techniques developed by the Student Team Learning Program at Johns Hopkins University are Teams-Games-Tournament (TGT), Student Team-Achievement Divisions (STAD), and Jigsaw.[3] Considerable research has been conducted comparing the team learning techniques to more conventional instruction. In general, the techniques have demonstrated superior positive effects on interpersonal concern, race relations, peer norms helpful in academic achievement, liking for others, and self-esteem. In some studies, academic achievement was the same regardless of whether team learning or conventional techniques were employed. The team learning techniques tend to be effective particularly with low achieving and minority students. Each of these outcomes is highly consistent with the goals of democratic teaching.

---

[3]The Team Learning Project of the Center for Social Organization of Schools at Johns Hopkins University has produced a variety of materials to assist teachers who want to use TGT, STAD, and Jigsaw. The most directly useful product for social studies teachers is *Using Student Team Learning*, by Robert Slavin, 1980. It is available for $2.00 from the Director, Team Learning Project, Center for Social Organization of Schools, The Johns Hopkins University, 3505 North Charles Street, Baltimore, MD 21218.

The Teams-Games-Tournament (TGT) technique groups students of mixed ability in teams of four or five members, who help each other to achieve instructional objectives. The teacher instructs the students, using whatever techniques are appropriate. Students study together in their teams using worksheets. Representatives of equal ability from each team compete in three-person academic tournaments at the end of each week. Each team member contributes his or her tournament score to the total team score. Additional rewards are made to those team members who perform unusually well within their ability levels. Competition among students of equal ability gives each a fair chance to contribute a high number of points to the team effort. If competition becomes unequal, students are shifted up or down in the ability hierarchy. A weekly newsletter is used to recognize outstanding student performance.

The Student Teams-Achievement Divisions (STAD) technique is very similar to Teams-Games-Tournament (TGT). The key difference is that individual student quizzes replace the tournaments. This simplifies implementing the team learning process at the cost of sacrificing some of the excitement. Both Teams-Games-Tournament and Student Teams-Achievement Divisions are most appropriate for knowledge, comprehension, and application instructional objectives.

Jigsaw involves assigning students to six-member teams; each student is responsible for a segment of a lesson. Students from different teams who are responsible for the same segment of a lesson meet in expert groups. In the expert groups, the team representatives study together and check each other's understanding of their common assignment. Next, each student teaches a lesson segment to his or her teammates. Each team member is dependent on all the others to help him or her combine the pieces of the lesson into a whole. Unlike the other two team techniques, students are rewarded for their quiz performances individually rather than collectively. Jigsaw is appropriate for analysis and synthesis, as well as lower cognitive instructional objectives.

In all three team learning techniques, students have important resources in the form of knowledge or access to "points" which they can choose to share or withhold. Since all the team members benefit from pooling their resources, strong norms for cooperation and individual achievement develop. Regardless of past academic performance, each team member can make a valuable contribution to the welfare of every other teammate and the group as a whole. Existing status systems are de-emphasized, although not eliminated. A very different one could emerge within a team and within a class that is more responsive to present individual performance. Research has revealed consistent positive effects on students' affective relationships. Social control issues seldom arise overtly, because students' expectations for cooperative behavior are strong. Team learning techniques used in conjunction with other instructional techniques can enhance student participation, influence, and academic achievement.

(13) *Emphasize status, decision-making, and cooperation and conflict in the curriculum whenever appropriate.*

The subject matter that students learn is likely to be of secondary importance in the process of democratizing a class. Status systems, decision-making procedures, affective relationships, and social control processes are incorporated into the ways people interact regardless of the tasks confronting them. However, what a class studies can provide some reinforcement and transfer of learning. If the curriculum enables students to comprehend what is going on in their relatively democratic class, then they are more likely to perceive democratic characteristics or their absence in other life situations. Without a conscious awareness of the dynamics of a democratic classroom, students might leave the classroom with only the vague feelings that something good but hard to explain had happened. Using the content of a course and the life of a class to reflect upon and clarify the other is consistent with the goal of democratizing the classroom.

In a government course, the decision-making procedures and rules of various decision-making bodies and individuals should be compared and contrasted. Why do some decisions in the Congress require a two-thirds majority rather than a simple majority? Why do some states have representation in the Congress that is disproportionately larger than their populations? Why are federal judges largely insulated from public opinion? What presidential decisions require little or no approval from the Congress? What social groups in the nation are under- or over-represented in proportion to their numbers? What factors affect the distribution of power and influence in the Congress? Answers to these questions can be discussed in relation to analogous decision-making and status systems in the classroom, school, and other immediate social environments.

In an economics class, the merits and demerits of cooperation and competition can be usefully explored. In an economic system where competition is valued as a necessary condition for individual and social progress, students should perceive that cooperation is the hallmark of efficient production and distribution of goods and services. On the other hand, cooperation in the form of price-fixing generates serious consequences for consumers. Students should be challenged to clarify how and when competition and cooperation are beneficial and harmful. A democratic class can serve as a useful analogy.

Sociology and psychology are the disciplines which contribute many of the concepts and much of the research which underlie the recommendations for democratizing the classroom. Numerous opportunities for identifying, clarifying, and applying ideas about status, decision-making, cooperation and conflict, affective relationships, and social control exist. A key insight which students should gain is that these social phenomena operate in a wide variety of social contexts, from face-to-face encounters between individuals to the interaction of nation-states.

In history courses, the expansion of the vote in the United States can be studied to explore how and why decision-making procedures change. The British social status system was not well-suited to circumstances in colonial America and helped to increase tensions leading to the American Revolution. Early United States history is replete with attempts to formalize more democratic decision-making and status systems. In world history, decision-making systems can be evaluated in light of questions people had to answer at various times and places. Also, comparisons of different systems can produce a general understanding of the positive and negative qualities of more and less democratic political systems.

One of the most useful curriculum emphases for a democratic classroom is controversial issues. The open examination of controversial issues can promote positive, democratic political attitudes. Also, a focus on issues provides excellent opportunities for the implementation of several recommendations already explained. Issues of morality and social responsibility, equality, welfare and security, consent, and property are easily related to the social and political dimensions of the classroom. Systematic discussion skills are consistent with and promote democratic experience in the classroom.

Thoughts on Becoming a More Democratic Teacher

If a teacher decides to transform his or her classroom into a more democratic learning environment, the chief obstacle will probably be the students. They are likely to applaud the idea of classroom and school democracy. However, most will have little idea of what it involves. Few classrooms and fewer schools are democratic in their operation. Consequently, students will be naive. Students usually expect and often want a teacher to be authoritarian, although in a benevolent way. Altering the classroom without altering students' expectations for themselves and the teacher is likely to produce confusion and disorder, rather than democracy.

In order to create a democratic classroom environment, a planned sequence of expanding democratic experiences will be necessary. The precise nature of the sequence will depend on a given teacher's experience, self-confidence, and skill in using group processes. It will also depend on the age, maturity, and social backgrounds of the students. Nevertheless, some rules of thumb can be offered.

It is usually a good idea to begin a course in a relatively authoritarian manner, while trying to communicate a spirit of high expectations, fairness, and enthusiasm. This will be necessary if students expect a teacher to be authoritarian. An effective authoritarian might be the definition of a "good teacher" for many students. If this is the case, the teacher will need to demonstrate that he or she can play the game. Then the teacher can begin to move the students toward a more democratic mode of operation. A teacher with a reputation as a strong teacher could possibly short-circuit this process and begin setting up a democratic class immediately. The key is to make sure students do not misperceive the teacher as weak and ineffectual.

Efforts to democratize a classroom can be evaluated in terms of student participation, the distribution of student influence, and academic achievement. A teacher will have impressions of the quality of these outcomes, but it might be useful to collect some data systematically for evaluation and planning purposes. Data on academic achievement will be readily available. Counting students' participatory acts and noting completed assignments will provide useful information. Sociometric questionnaires can provide insights into student relationships. Ask students to list three or four students who can usually get others to do things, or three or four who cannot. Which students are most and least liked? Which students make the best and worst work partners? If the students' choices are fairly well dispersed compared to an earlier time or to other classes, then progress is being made.

Implementing the recommendations for democratizing the classroom will facilitate the actualization of the central values of a democratic learning environment. Students will have fairly equal opportunities to learn. The welfare of each individual student will be a high priority of the students and the class activities. Rewards and penalties will be responsive to individual effort and performance in spite of status considerations. Each individual will be held responsible by the other students as well as the teacher for affecting the welfare of others. Students who experience these values in the classroom will be more likely to act on them outside the school and later in life. Knowledge, skills, and attitudes will be taught which will promote each individual's welfare and the welfare of the classroom group and larger society, which in the long run will enhance the well-being of each individual.

Bibliography

Aronson, E., Bridgeman, D., and Geffner, R. Interdependent interactions and prosocial behavior. *Journal of Research and Development in Education, 12*(1), 16–27, 1978.

Beyer, B.K., and Brostoff, A. The time it takes: Managing/evaluating writing and social studies. *Social Education, 43*(3), 194–197, 1979.

Bossert, S.T. *Tasks and social relationships in classrooms*. Cambridge, England: Cambridge University Press, 1979.

Brophy, J.E., and Good, T.L. *Teacher-student relationships*. New York: Holt, Rinehart and Winston, 1974.

Caramia, J.A., Jr., and Knight, C.L. Group processes in teaching social studies: An instructional unit. *Georgia Social Science Journal, 11* (2) 15 and 17, 1980.

Cohen, E.G., and Sharen, S. *Modifying status relations in Israeli youth*. Paper Cooperation: A field experiment. *Sociology of Education, 49*(1), 47–58, 1976.

Cohen, E.G., and Sharen, S. *Modifying status relations in Israeli youth*. Paper presented at the meeting of the American Educational Research Association, New York, 1977.

DeVries, D., and Slavin, R. Teams-Games-Tournament (TGT): Review of ten classroom experiments. *Journal of Research and Development in Education, 12*(1), 28–38, 1978.

Ehman, L.H. Implications for teaching citizenship. *Social Education, 43*(7), 594–596, 1979.

Good, T.L., Sikes, J.N., and Brophy, J.E. Effects of teacher sex, student sex, and student achievement on classroom interaction. *Journal of Educational Psychology, 65,* 74–87, 1973.

Hunt, M.P., and Metcalf, L.E. *Teaching high school social studies*. 2nd edition. New York: Harper and Row, 1968.

Newmann, F.M., and Oliver, D. *Clarifying public controversy*. Boston: Little, Brown and Company, 1970.

Oliver, D., and Shaver, J.P. *Teaching public issues in the high schools*. Boston: Houghton Mifflin Company, 1966.

Rist, R. Student social class and teacher expectations: The self-fulfilling prophecy in ghetto education. *Harvard Educational Review, 40,* 411–451, 1970.

Rothbart, M., Dalfen, S., and Barrett, R. Effects of teacher's expectancy on student-teacher interaction. *Journal of Educational Psychology, 62,* 49–54, 1971.

Schmuck, R. A. Sociometric status and utilization of academic abilities. *Merrill-Palmer Quarterly, 8,* 165–172, 1962.

Schmuck, R.A., and Schmuck, P.A. *Group processes in the classroom*. 3rd edition. Dubuque, Iowa: William C. Brown, 1979.

Shaver, J.P., and Larkins, A.G. *Decision-making in a democracy*. Boston: Houghton Mifflin, 1973.

Simon, S.B., Howe, L.W., and Kirschenbaum, H. *Values clarification: A handbook of practical strategies for teachers and students*. New York: Hart Publishing Company, 1972.

Slavin, R. Student teams and achievement divisions. *Journal of Research and Development in Education, 12*(1), 39–49, 1978.

Slavin, R. *Using Student Team Learning.* Baltimore: The Johns Hopkins University, Center for Social Organization of Schools, 1980.

Smith, B.D. Responding effectively to incorrect answers. *The Social Studies, 72* (2), 56–60, 1981.

VanSickle, R.L. Neutralizing status constraints on student performance in small group activities. *Theory and Research in Social Education, 7*(2), 1–33, 1979.

Democracy in the classroom is a matter of degree. . . . Rather than attempt to set up an ideal democratic classroom, it will be more useful for teachers to think about how to move from a less democratic position on the continuum to a more democratic one.

CHAPTER FIVE

The School Society:
Practical Suggestions for Promoting
a Democratic School Climate

Michael A. Radz

Case A

A group of eighth-grade students in a medium sized K–8 school decided that they would like to have a student council. Although the possibility of forming such a body had been discussed in previous years, it had never been pursued. Up to this time, none of the teachers had been particularly supportive, and the principal had let it be known that he saw no need for a student council.

This group of students, however, was not content with a situation in which they had no formal way to participate in decisions about life in the school. Therefore, they prepared a petition requesting that the principal consider organizing a student government. The petition was circulated to students in the fifth through the eighth grade. Nearly all signed.

Upon receiving the petition, the principal curtly said that he did not view the petition as legitimate, and that the students would be far better off if they left the running of the school to him. One student spoke up, saying that petition was a right guaranteed in the Bill of Rights. "True," replied the principal, "But that only applies to adults. Students aren't responsible enough to exercise all these American rights."

The students decided that it was hopeless to pursue the issue.

Case B

The administration of a 1,200-pupil high school granted students a great deal of freedom. There were no bells, passes, or study halls. A self-scheduling procedure allowed the students to draw up their own daily schedules, rather than having them generated by a computer. The principal and assistant principal were accessible to students and staff, spending much of their time in the halls, classrooms, library, and cafeteria. Although there were occasional misunderstandings, by and large the inhabitants of the building were comfortable with each other.

During the third year of this administration, a problem arose which had the potential of creating a backlash and transforming the school into a more rigidly run institution. Cutting of classes reached epidemic proportions. One of the few school rules required students to be in class when scheduled, but many students and teachers were flagrantly ignoring this responsibility. As a result, in many cases, instruction was being disrupted, parents were complaining, and the superintendent and school board were demanding that the situation be rectified immediately.

The principal and assistant developed and implemented this plan:

(1) A faculty meeting was called for the purpose of clarifying the problem, i.e., exactly what was happening, how extensive it was, and to what extent it was interfering with learning and the overall school environment.

(2) All English teachers were asked to bring their classes to the small auditorium for a meeting with the administration. Since all students were required to take English, every member of the student body would be involved.

(3) At the student meetings, the principal described the nature of the problem and indicated that something had to be done. Student comments and ideas were solicited and recorded.

(4) An ad hoc committee made up of students, teachers, staff, parents, and administration was formed to review all the input and develop a written set of alternatives for solving the problem.

(5) After the alternatives were received by the principal, he had them reproduced and distributed to all students, faculty, and staff.

(6) The entire student body was assembled in the gym, where the principal and the ad hoc committee answered questions about alternative solutions.

(7) A referendum on the alternatives was held, with all teachers, students, and staff members having a vote.

(8) A solution emerged and was drafted into a policy statement which was distributed within the school, to parents, and to the central office and school board.

Class attendance was increased from 65 percent per class period to 98 percent.

Both of these cases involve basic democratic values—the right to petition and popular sovereignty or involvement in the decision-making process. Students learned important lessons about democracy, but the lessons were very different. In both situations, however, the principal—not a social studies teacher or a textbook on American government—was the "instructor."

Democratic citizenship education cannot be left to chance. The only realistic approach is one which systematically integrates the formal, hidden, and societal curricula, and any consideration of merging the three curricula of citizenship education must of necessity begin with the school principal.

Conventional wisdom as well as a wealth of research places the principal at the center of any serious effort at change. The principal holds the key, and if the hidden curriculum is to be unlocked, it is the principal who can do it. As John Goodlad (1979) observed, "[The principal] far more than any other person shapes and articulates the prevailing ambiance and creates a sense of mission." Consciously or unconsciously, the principal sets the climate in the school and in so doing determines the extent to which it can function as a laboratory for living and learning democratic values. The autocratic principal who distrusts teachers, parents, and students, relies exclusively on personal counsel, denies due process, and severs all lines of communication will create a climate of distrust, suspicion, subterfuge, and despair. On the other hand, a principal's "relaxed, open, and secure manner" will permeate the staff and infect students (Holman, 1980, pp. 23–24).

The Principal: A Person Under Pressure

To be an open, but secure, school principal is no easy task. The principal is the focus of a host of pressures — external, internal, and personal. How the individual copes with these pressures will be determined to a large extent, by his or her perception of the leadership role, which, in turn, determines how he or she will behave. Administrative attitudes and behavior set the climate in the school building.

While the external pressures may vary from community to community, the sources are similar: parents, the community, the courts, the state legislature, and teachers' unions. Parents, of course, have traditionally had a vested interest in the schools. However, during the last ten years, the annual Gallup Poll of Public Attitudes Toward Education has shown that parents have been losing confidence in the schools. They have also become more aggressive in their efforts to influence the operation of the schools and the curriculum offered their children. Principals spend considerable time responding to telephone calls from parents, meeting with formal and informal groups, and holding conferences with parents. Not all such contacts are negative. Many are rewarding, but the fact remains that the principal is conscious that parents are watching, listening, and talking about the school.

The community at large also has a vested interest in schooling. Aside from contributing tax dollars, the community views schools as a reflection of itself. Good schools attract good people to the community, and provide a continuing source of qualified labor and community leadership. Good schools are a source of civic pride. Therefore, various groups within the community, like civic groups and business organizations, keep watch on the schools, and will, when concerned, pick up the telephone and call the principal. It is safe to say that all principals know that they, the staff, and the building are under close scrutiny by the community.

Many principals are deeply concerned and frustrated by the judicial system, which, in recent years, has exerted considerable influence over the operation of the schools. At local levels, principals find that juvenile courts with their heavy dockets are unable to respond with the speed that is often desperately required. Supreme Court decisions such as the Tinker case, *Goss v. Lopez, Ingraham v. Wright,* and numerous others have greatly influenced the manner in which schools are run.

The state and federal government continues to issue mandates, rules, and regulations, the implementation of which ultimately comes to be the principal's responsibility. At the state level, minimum competency testing legislation is but the most recent example of a mandated change. Title IX and P.L. 94-142, which require a free and appropriate education for the handicapped, are representative of federal legislation which has forced principals to reassess and, in many cases, revise programs in their schools. Far too often, such changes are accompanied by short time lines, burdensome paper work, and little or no funding.

Teachers' unions have further complicated the principal's job. Often, principals feel that the local board of education has "given away the store" as a result of concessions made in collective bargaining. Authority, once in the hands of the principal, is now restricted by the terms of the negotiated contract. For many principals, hearing grievances has become a part of the daily routine and yet another source of external pressure.

Internal pressures come from the school system and the school. The principal must deal with the board of education and the central office, teachers, non-certificated staff, and students. A principal's interactions with all of these shape his or her administrative behavior. In most school districts, the principal is directly responsible to the superintendent. At best, the superintendent views the principal as an integral member of a district-wide management team and seeks to involve him or her in the decision-making process. In such a system, the principal can contribute to district-level decision. The other extreme is the superintendent who requires that authority, information, and communication flow from the central office downward through the school system. In this system, the principal is an extension of the superintendent and feels free to do only what is authorized. Either situation, and all those in between, places demands on the principal.

Teachers and other staff are the principal's responsibility. Normally the school administrator will be called upon to assess their performance and since they are all individuals, each with a unique background, personality, method of operation, and set of needs, inevitably there will be cooperation and conflicts, laughter and tears, high points and low points. One thing is certain, the principal can expect that the workday will be punctuated with direct contact with members of the staff, and because schooling is a human enterprise, the quality of these contacts will define the climate in that building. For example, some principals thrive on being with young people and give this interaction top priority. Others are intimidated and find ways to isolate themselves. At one end of the spectrum is the gregarious principal who is in the halls, the classrooms, and the cafeteria; at the ball games; and out talking with students. This principal genuinely likes young people and enjoys contact with them. At the other end, there is the principal who spends much time making out reports and performing routine managerial tasks, leaving interaction with students to the assistant principal and the teachers. The implications for school climate are obvious.

For many school principals, the specter of violence and vandalism is all too real. The threat of physical harm to either property or people obviously creates a situation which can make meaningful classroom learning all but impossible.

The magnitude of the problem was made public in 1975 when the Senate Subcommittee To Investigate Juvenile Delinquency, chaired by Senator Birch Bayh of Indiana, released its preliminary report: *Our Nation's Schools—A Report Card: "A" in School Violence and Vandalism.* This report and follow-up studies conducted by the National Center for Education Studies and the National Institute for Education provided a flood of statistics which collectively painted a picture that horrified the American public. While many school administrators were quick to point out that "safe" schools outnumber the violent ones, it had to be admitted that daily life for many teachers, students, and administrators in too many schools is characterized by threats, intimidation, and overt criminal action. Again, the individual who is ultimately held responsible for such situations is the principal.

While the causes of school violence and vandalism vary considerably, the most commonly mentioned include:
- a general upsurge in crime committed by youth.
- deteriorating living conditions in many large cities, accompanied by "white flight" to the suburbs.
- easy availability of drugs and guns.
- excessive violence on television.
- a decline in discipline.

- changes in the attitudes of teachers, parents, and administrators, particularly with regard to responsibility for the behavior of youth.
- a belief among some educators that extension of student rights by the courts tied their hands in handling student disciplinary matters.
- neglect of "hard-core" youth.
- faults within the schools themselves, e.g., depersonalization; large size; excessive use of corporal punishment, suspension, and expulsion; unequal treatment; doing too little too late to help many children.

The problem is a complex one, linked to economic, social, and political conditions in the school community and the nation. However, when emotionally distraught parents, students, and school board members look for someone to blame, it is often the principal who is cited when law and order in a school breaks down. Among the solutions recommended are security systems, counseling services, improved curricular and instructional programs, and changes in school organization (Neill, 1978).

Whichever approaches are employed to improve security and productivity in the school, the principal has the responsibility for implementing the program. The keys to success appear to lie in (1) the extent to which the principal is able to involve students, parents, teachers, community officials and law enforcement personnel directly in a joint effort to improve the school, and (2) the principal's leadership style. The principal's leadership must be visible, firm, empathetic, and fair.

The growing number of articles in the literature on principal stress and administrator "burn-out" attest to the fact that the principal's position is a pressure-laden one. In addition to the pressures internal and external to the school system, there is an intra-personal dimension created by the demands which the individual administrator places on himself or herself. It is fair to say that the majority of principals are ill-prepared to assume the position on the basis of their experiences and academic training. Most were at one time classroom teachers, and as such developed narrow perceptions of the principal's role. This image was formed almost exclusively from experiences with their own principal(s). Once behind the principal's desk, the former teacher frequently finds that previous perceptions do not square with reality.

Presumably, the would-be administrator has completed the necessary graduate work to qualify for an administrative certificate. However, classwork in the comfortable confines of the university seldom prepares a person fully for the frustrations of life in the principal's office. As in most professions, a person learns what a job entails through on-the-job training. Thus, from the very outset, the principal is likely to experience feelings of personal and professional inadequacy. For many, this will disappear with experience; for others, it is a constant, gnawing sensation that intensifies over time.

Principals have private lives, too. They have spouses, children, homes, parents, friends, and informal and formal organizations to which they belong. Serving as a principal often requires evenings at school related-functions and frequent absence from home and family. When the principal is at home, there will be phone calls—not all of them pleasant. Many principals open their eyes one day to realize that while they have been busy with other people's children, their own have grown up. Conflicting role demands can cause a great deal of stress.

Given the many demands on and the often contradictory expectations of the principal, is it any wonder that many principals have difficulty defining their exact role? It has been argued that the major single reason for the failure of the effectiveness of administrators is failure to clarify priorities in their own minds (Combs, 1970). This is understandable. At the same time, however, the principal must ultimately make decisions about priorities, even if the decisions are to do nothing. Each decision, regardless of the issue, has a profound effect on the climate of the school. However numerous and great the pressures, the principal is assuredly the leader in the school. The effectiveness of this leadership in promoting democratic schooling depends heavily upon the principal's perception of how to lead.

A Climate Maker

The superintendent, principal, and/or new teachers can transform a school from a place of grim despair to one of joy and spontaneity. The same could be said for a change in the socioeconomic composition of the neighborhood, court-ordered busing, or even a coat of paint. As stated in the introduction to this Bulletin, the climate of the school, like weather, does have an effect on the inhabitants. Unlike the weather, however, educators can do something about a school's climate. While research is just beginning to identify meaningful patterns of relationships, those who spend time daily in the schools can attest to the impact that the climate has on how they feel, how they perform, and how they grow as individuals.

Exactly what is meant by the phrase "school climate"? Ronald C. Doll (1972) states, "the climate of a school is considered to be its 'feel,' . . . conditions of life and learning, the behavior of teachers and other non-administrative personnel, and the performance of principals and supervisors." According to Ehman, climate refers to *how* things are done in the whole school and specific classes rather than *what* is done (Ehman, 1980). School climate is to a certain extent intangible attitudes and perceptions. At the same time, it produces something that is observable and hence can be assessed (Fox, 1974). The climate is indeed a changeable condition.

The principal as the school's leader is a key figure in the determination of the climate. Therefore, it stands to reason that he or she has a major influence on the hidden curriculum. Phillip Jackson (1968) in his significant work, *Life in Classrooms,* suggests that there are three key components of the hidden curriculum—praise, power, and crowds. Power refers to the exercise of authority by those adults in the school who are in positions of authority. Jackson defines praise, or the lack of it, as the evaluative dimensions which is a factor in daily life in the classroom. Crowds are the other inhabitants of the building—the mini-societies which have most of the characteristics of the larger community. It is these forces which teach children who they are in relation to other people. As Jackson points out, there is nothing inherently wrong with power, praise, or crowds; it is how they operate and are applied to people that is significant.

Applying these constructs to the principal's role, few would question that it is the principal's responsibility to maintain control in his or her school building. However, the lessons that students learn from a firm, but fair principal are far different from those learned from one who views personal authority as absolute. The firm, fair, democratic principal models such principles as the rule of law, justice, and the rights of the individual. The autocratic principal leads children to believe that blind obedience and conformity are valued behaviors. The same is true of praise. The principal who is conscious of the significance of the evaluative function knows full well that it can be used in positive ways to foster individual growth. Its abuse, on the other hand, can instill the fear of failure in children and adults, stifling creativity, risk-taking, and individual initiative. School climate is a function of how things are done, rather than what is written or spoken.

Recommendations for Principals

What can the principal and other administrators do to develop a more democratic atmosphere? How can administrators create a positive, humane climate in the school building, and make it a laboratory for learning and living democratic principles and practices? Any principal genuinely interested in leading a democratic school must begin with the recognition that the meaningful involvement of individuals and groups of students, teachers, and staff is the foundation for building such an institution. The principal is the key figure, but he or she cannot operate in isolation. The following recommendations are directed to principals. However, implicit in them is the recognition that principals should view their roles as interactive, and that other administrators, as well as teachers and staff, also can play a significant part in promoting democratic schooling.

Recommendation 1: Know Thyself

It is good practice for any administrator to engage in an ongoing process of self-assessment. While few principals would claim to be anything but advocates for the democratic way of life, there are those who have never thought seriously about how to implement that view. There are also those who feel that it is impossible to run a truly democratic school. Perhaps they believe that the students are not interested in being involved, that the teachers expect the principal to make the decisions, or that the community wants the students to be closely supervised. On the other hand, such a principal may be what McGregor (1960) labelled a Theory X manager. According to McGregor this individual has a generally pessimistic view of human beings and their capacity for self-direction. The Theory X administrator believes that since individuals are basically lazy and apathetic, they have to be closely supervised because they cannot be trusted to perform their required duties. Principals with such an orientation would see themselves as *the* leaders whose job it is to keep people in line through coercion and the close monitoring of behavior. Communication flows in one direction only—from the principal's office down into the classroom. The norms are obedience, conformity, and control. The climate in a school administered by a principal who has a Theory X orientation is likely to be closed, impersonal, cautious, and stifling to both teachers and students and restrictive to cognitive and affective growth.

There is the other side of the coin, which McGregor calls a Theory Y manager. A theory Y principal has a much more optimistic view of people and sees them as being curious, interested in new ways of doing their tasks, and capable of being self-directed. McGregor does not imply that people do not want or need direction or that a *laissez-faire* administrative posture should be assumed. Theory Y asserts that people function best when provided with both freedom and responsibility. There is a need for rules and regulations, but they can and should be developed collaboratively. It is obvious that a Theory Y school will have a quite different climate from one that has a Theory X orientation.

James Sweeney (1982) completed an extensive review of the literature on effective schools and identified the following common findings regarding the leadership role of the principal.

The Principal

A. Sets Instructional Strategies

1. Makes decisions regarding instruction and provides appropriate direction to the staff relative to their implementation.
2. Has and articulates a philosophy of education.

3. Establishes building-wide goals—e.g., "We are going to work to improve the writing skills of all students."
4. Develops a systematic program aimed at helping students who are having trouble learning.

B. Emphasizes Achievement
1. Sets standards of excellence and demands that they be met.
2. Discusses student achievement in meetings called for the purpose.
3. Rewards individual student achievement.
4. Evaluates the achievement of instructional objectives.
5. Facilitates staff development.
6. Communicates achievements to the parents and community.
7. Demonstrates effectiveness in supervising and evaluating teachers.

C. Coordinates the Instructional Program
1. Holds frequent meetings (grade level, department, primary-intermediate-junior high).
2. Makes certain that the district's curricula are being implemented.
3. Makes media and material available to staff after determining its relationship to the instructional program.

D. Evaluates Pupil Progress Frequently
1. Makes use of norm-referenced and criterion-referenced test data.
2. Scrutinizes grade reports.
3. Gives teachers feedback on pupil progress.
4. Publicizes the results of pupil evaluation.

E. Supports Teachers
1. Makes frequent informal visits to all classrooms.
2. Provides the faculty with resources, books, materials, etc.
3. Makes note of specific staff contributions.

F. Promotes a Positive School Climate
1. Maintains an orderly, but not rigid environment.
2. Emphasizes quiet, but not repressive conditions.
3. Finds ways to involve students, staff, and parents in decisions about the school.
4. Is "quietly everywhere."
5. Requires group-based discipline standards ("we").
6. Facilitates a caring, friendly relationship among all members of the school community.

By virtue of position and title, the principal is a leader. However, it is a combination of the principal's perception of that role and his or her skills that will shape the principal's leadership. "Leadership for climate improvement requires skills in responding to concerns, expectations, and existing conditions or initiating new expectations and conditions" (Kelley, 1980, p. 33). In order to improve a school's climate, the principal should be:

- aware of the conditions and events that influence personal attitudes, beliefs, and behaviors.
- alert to the conditions and events that influence professional attitudes, beliefs, and behaviors.
- aware of the expectations of others and sensitive to whether or not those expectations are understood.
- aware of the responses to conditions or events that cannot be controlled, but must be encountered and addressed.
- able to plan, initiate, and implement events or changes that influence conditions which can be controlled.
- able to formulate long-range plans for the maintenance and improvement of conditions and events which influence the quality of outcomes attained by students. (Kelley, 1980, p. 33)

In summary, Kelley asserts that "an individual's ability to be an effective leader for climate development is dependent upon conditions one experiences and the conditions one creates." Not only is the principal an inhabitant of a particular physical environment—the school building—but he or she has also developed a value system which exercises a powerful influence over the way in which skills are brought to bear on a given situation. Self-awareness is a critical first step in being an effective climate leader. Principals who know "where they are coming from," are optimistic, realistic, and patient. Those who possess the human relations skills most closely associated with democratic values are in a position to improve school climate.

The point is this: principals must constantly reexamine their views of people and check them against the way they actually treat people on the job. It is easy for a principal to say, "Of course I trust the people in this building." However, it may not be so easy for this principal to demonstrate trust by relinquishing some traditional powers and actively involving teachers in making decisions that affect the operation of the building. Self-analysis is frequently a painful process, but it should be an integral part of the administrator's professional and personal development.

Recommendation 2: Conceptualize the Democratic School

What would a democratic school look like in operation? What would people be doing? How would they behave? These are important questions for the principal to consider. There is no problem identifying the basic democratic values. The Salt Lake City District (Riddick, 1979), for example lists the following:

1. Each individual has dignity and the potential for growth.
2. A free society requires respect for persons, property, and principles.
3. Each individual has a right to learn and should have the freedom to achieve.
4. Each individual, regardless of race, creed, color, sex, ethnic background, or economic status, should have equal opportunity.
5. Each individual has the right to personal liberties.
6. Each individual is responsible for his or her own actions.
7. Each individual is responsible to the group as well as to the total society.
8. Democratic societies are based on law.
9. Problems should be solved through reason and orderly processes.
10. Democratic governments are governed by majority vote.
11. An individual should be tolerant of others' religious beliefs and should have the freedom to exercise his or her own.
12. Each individual has the right to work and to gain satisfaction from personal effort.

A shorter list which encompasses most of the above is suggested by Fenton (1977). Based on Kohlberg's work, he offers the following list of democratic values: justice, the dignity and worth of the individual, equality, liberty commensurate with the equal liberty of all others, and the greatest good for the greatest number.

Starting with a specific definition of basic democratic values, the principal then needs to make the meaning of these characteristics "operational" within the school building. For example, "justice" in operation means that all people in the school would be granted due process; punishment would not be administered capriciously and arbitrarily; the accused would have the right to tell their side of the story; all rules and regulations would be clearly articulated, etc. Again, this recommendation does not imply that the principal should act alone. The more people are involved in contributing to the school mini-society, the more democratic the approach will be.

Recommendation 3: Make Decisions Collaboratively

As is the case with classic bureaucracies, decision-making in many schools is typically an administrative function with little or no direct involvement of people at the lowest levels of the hierarchy. There is a direct relationship between the extent to which individuals are meaningfully involved in decisions which have an immediate bearing on their daily lives and the openness of the school. The higher the level of involvement, the more positively teachers, students, parents, and support staff view the school. Shared decision-making does not mean that the principal must relinquish all authority. Legally, as well as practically, it is not possible for the principal to turn over the operation of the school completely to its inhabitants. There are some decisions which cannot be delegated to others. On the other hand, a vehicle for involving the various constituencies is absolutely essential if the principal is serious about teaching democratic principles and practices in the school. Opening up the decision-making process will allow the principal and the school to have greater access to teacher and student resources and to obtain a deeper involvement and commitment from the school's participants (Schmuck and Schmuck, 1974).

There are two corollaries to this recommendation. Active involvement of all groups in the decision-making process requires an open system of communication. Information must be made available to those who have the responsibility for making the decision. The administrator will have to see to it that communication flows both horizontally and vertically throughout the organizational structure of the school. He or she will have to perfect the art of active listening in order to facilitate the flow of information from the grass roots upward and outward.

Secondly, issues of controversy in the school must be openly discussed. If teachers and students are involved only in decisions that they perceive as insignificant, they will feel patronized and will quickly retreat. Decisions that affect large numbers of people are bound to be controversial. They require a full and open discussion so that alternatives and possible consequences can be scrutinized. The principal has to learn to manage controversy in such a way that it becomes a positive rather than a destructive force. The principal as a democratic leader must learn when to be non-judgmental and when to be assertive, and when to encourage additional input and when to move toward closure.

Recommendation 4: Give Responsibility To Teach Responsibility

Responsibility is a learned behavior. Like so many other concepts, responsibility is learned through experience and not through preaching and lofty pronouncements. Responsibility is an overworked word. It is used frequently both in and out of school, and hence its meaning is often obscured and almost always colored by the context in which it is used. Nevertheless, if the principal expects students, teachers, and others to act in a responsible manner, they must be given responsibility. This is risky because mistakes are likely and consequences will have to be faced. There will be a strong temptation for principals to rescue the individual—to take the responsibility "off the individual's back," and place it on their own. Rescuing relieves the individual of responsibility and thus fosters dependency rather than independence. For example, corporal punishment rescues students, in that the offender, once paddled, has no obligation to change his or her behavior. Likewise, handing a student a list of rules developed by the teacher or principal rescues the student from the responsibility of having a stake in the rules. The rewards of granting responsibility are worth the risk, for democratic participation flourishes when individuals assume responsibility for their own personal and social behavior.

Recommendation 5: Model the Democratic Principles That You Are Seeking To Foster

If we accept the proposition that the principal shapes the climate in the school building, it follows that he or she is a powerful role model for students, teachers, staff, and community. While most principals are conscious of this, it is easy to minimize or forget the impact that modeling has on adults as well as children. The principal must begin by recognizing that actions are likely to speak louder than words. Preaching democracy while practicing autocracy will foster cynicism, suspicion, and even contempt. Moreover, as was noted above, the final result for the school is an atmosphere of fear, distrust, and irresponsibility. Thus, the principal needs to assess his or her personal behavior and interactions as an administrator and consider how they demonstrate basic democratic values. The following goal statements and personal assessment questions might help the principal to answer the question:

What expectations do I have for students in this school to become more responsible citizens?

Goal Statement
I want all students to be self-actualizing, life-long learners who can identify and organize their own learning needs, resources, and learning styles—i.e., *responsible learners*.

Q. What can I as a principal and a person do to model this type of behavior for students?

Q. What specific provisions am I making in my role as principal of this school to foster this kind of student behavior?

Goal Statement
I want all students to be aware, active, responsible citizens, who value their own freedom and prize diversity in others—i.e., *responsible citizens*.

Q. What can I as a principal and as a person do to model this type of behavior for students?

Q. What specific provisions am I making in my role as principal of this school to foster this kind of student behavior?

Goal Statement
I want all students to be open, divergent, critical thinkers who can select and

analyze relevant data, recognize alternatives, develop personal values, and make decisions—i.e., *responsible decision-makers.*

Q. What can I as a principal and a person do to model this type of behavior for my students?

Q. What specific provisions am I making in my role as principal of this school to foster this kind of student behavior?

Goal Statement
I want all my students to be caring, cooperative, supportive human beings—i.e., *responsible human beings.*

Q. What can I as a principal and a person do to model this type of behavior for students?

Q. What specific provisions am I making in my role as principal of this school to foster this kind of student behavior?

Recommendation 6: Provide Outreach Options

What a child learns about democracy in school is but a single dimension of a total educative process. Basic democratic concepts are formed and developed as a result of the child's observing and participating in family life, clubs and organizations, and informal peer groups, while being exposed to the mass media, especially television. Rather than ignoring what has been called the societal curriculum, the school should actively attempt to close the gap between what is taught in the classroom and the school building and what is happening in the outside world. Educators can take the initiative and establish open lines of communication with other youth-serving organizations. For example, if a school has committed itself to the concept of the school as a laboratory for democracy, it is important that clergy, law enforcement officials, scout leaders, and others know exactly what this means in theory and practice. Common goals can thus be identified and determinations made as to how each agent can reinforce the other.

Secondly, students need firsthand experience with community citizenship opportunities. They need to see how those responsible for making a democracy work do their jobs. They need to talk with elected officials, bureaucrats, political leaders, law enforcement people, lawyers, lobbyists, the leaders of citizen involvement groups, journalists, and others. Guest speakers in the classroom can broaden students' perspectives, but much more can be gained by having students visit these people where they work or through an extended internship experience.

Recommendation 7: Have a Specific Plan of Governance

The school is a rule-governed institution. Rules and regulations are absolutely essential in order to provide an environment in which students can live and learn together peacefully, humanely, and with order. A school which is governed democratically is one in which rules, decisions, and problems are approached cooperatively rather than unilaterally. A structure is provided which allows input, involvement, and interaction by those most directly affected. Various models have been suggested. JoAnn Shaheen (1980), for example, describes the operation of the Little and the Big Student Advisory Council at the Cottage Lane Elementary School, a K–6 school in Blauvelt, New York. Students at all grade levels are actively involved in making and changing rules, arriving at decisions, and assuming responsibility for these decisions.

A different model of school governance at the elementary level is suggested by Louis and Barbara Fischer (1980). They suggest an ad hoc problem-oriented approach, as opposed to a permanent governing body. Whenever a school-wide concern surfaces, representatives from each classroom are selected to meet together and work out a solution. The other students become involved as their representative carries information to and from school-wide problem-solving meetings.

Perhaps the most widely publicized efforts in recent years have been based on Lawrence Kohlberg's "just community" concept (Fenton, 1977; Mosher, 1979). Separate high school projects under the direction of Ralph Mosher and Edwin Fenton have set up models of self-governing schools-within-a-school in which there are community meetings, a discipline committee, a curriculum which incorporates moral dilemmas, and an in-service program for teachers.

There have been other notable efforts, several described in Chapters Three and Six. The common elements, however, are easily identified. First of all, they are based, either implicitly or explicitly, on the assumption that students are already citizens and hence have both rights and responsibilities. Secondly, decisions are made by those who are most directly affected. There is a mechanism for making and changing rules which clearly involves the students. The hidden curriculum is recognized, legitimized, and brought out into the open. It is merged with the formal and the societal curricula to provide a comprehensive, consistent, and relevant citizenship education experience. Finally, all adults in the school are made aware of their significance as role models.

Teachers Share the Leadership

As part of the school, the classroom contributes to the overall sociopolitical climate in the building. The teacher plays a major role in determining the quality of life in the classroom. Thus, much of what has been said in regard to the knowledge, attitudes, and skills required of the principal applies as well to the teacher. There are many ways in which teachers can help principals to make the school a place where democracy is learned.

Effective teachers recognize that they are accountable for the climate in their classrooms, and they realize that, regardless of what else is happening in the school, when the door of the classroom closes they have an opportunity and a duty to provide an environment in which children can learn in safety and security. A principal should appeal to teachers to help to provide democratic learning experiences. The following outline suggests ways in which a teacher can work *deliberately* to create a democratic classroom environment and thus teach democratic skills and attitudes (Grambs, Carr, and Fitch, 1970):

> ***Build Awareness:*** It is important that the students be aware of the teachers' intention to make the classroom a model democracy. This includes, but is not limited to the development and use of an appropriate vocabulary and the sharing of the rationale behind various practices and structures.

> ***Promote Involvement:*** Of equal importance is the need to involve students directly and actively in the establishment of democratic classrooms.

Components:

A. Choice
1. Students need to be provided with alternatives. Teachers should help students to generate their own alternatives. This applies to formal instruction as well as social situations.
2. Choices must be meaningful to the students, i.e., they must see the options as being important.
3. Once a choice is made, it s the teacher's job to see that the parties involved follow through. This, of course, includes the consequences that result from the decision.

B. Freedom
1. Regular classroom meetings, or some other vehicle to promote open discussion, must be provided. The teacher's role is to facilitate, question, and clarify—not to pass judgement.
2. There must be a system of making and changing rules in the classroom which directly involves the students.
3. Within limits that are deemed appropriate, students should be able to move freely about the classroom. It is important, of course, that the rights of others, including the teacher, are respected.

C. Participation
1. Students should be given an opportunity to assume various kinds of responsibilities in the classroom.
2. Where and when appropriate, students should have an opportunity to assist in planning instructional and non-instructional activities in the classroom. Again, some type of vehicle like a classroom meeting will be needed.
3. Students should be given opportunities to evaluate activities. Depending on the situation, these could be informal (class and/or individual discussion) or formal (completion of a questionnaire).

D. Responsibility
1. Opportunities should be provided for students to experience various types of roles—leader, group member, worker, researcher, teacher, etc.
2. Once a decision—whether by a group, class, or individual—is made, the teacher should see to it that those concerned follow through.
3. Volunteering should be encouraged and rewarded.

E. Recognition of Human Dignity and Individual Worth
1. Positive reinforcement for appropriate behavior must be provided.
2. Students should have opportunities to share special interests or talents
3. The teacher should use formal curriculum to recognize the contributions of various groups and individuals to American society and the global community.

F. Relevance
1. The teacher should relate subject matter to life in the school, community, state, nation, and world, without neglecting the vicarious world of television and popular music.
2. The teacher should raise issues that deal with basic democratic values—justice, fairness, the rule of law, freedom and responsibility, majority rule, compromise, the rights of the minority, orderly dissent, and the worth of all people. Encourage the open discussion of controversial topics, particularly those that relate directly to the students and/or their immediate interests.

Other Suggestions for Teachers:
• foster the idea that citizenship education is the responsibility of every adult in the school. This includes the clerical staff, custodians, cafeteria

workers, aides and volunteers, bus drivers, and media center personnel. Find ways to inform and involve them.
- law-related education in some schools has been found to have a positive effect on student behavior. Find out more about law-related education and how you can integrate it into the existing curriculum.
- encourage faculty in-service programs aimed at improving classroom climate. Such sessions should be short and followed by intra-school classroom visits, thus providing practice and feedback opportunities.
- select a decision-making model. Teach it to your students. Use it in actual classroom situations.
- stress cooperation; don't dwell on competition.
- follow through on the concept of the classroom as a community. Have children function as "workers" in the "community." Develop an economic system. Vote. Set up rules. Have a judicial system.
- suggest a faculty retreat—a time and a place away from the school itself. Discuss with colleagues ways to improve school climate.

Summary

On the basis of their research, Goodlad and his associates (1974) advanced the argument that the individual school building, including its inhabitants and community, is the single most significant unit for enduring change in education. It is here that people live and learn as they interact with each other, the formal curriculum, and the societal curriculum. The school, in the words of Ralph Tyler (1977), "can provide a setting in which young people can experience concretely the meaning of our democratic ideals." It is in school that students have a chance to experience a society where justice and fairness prevail and where caring and cooperation are practiced and valued.

Unfortunately, we are educating large numbers of students whose commitment to democratic values and our political system is shallow, simply because they have not had democratic experiences in their daily lives in school. Far too often, the school appears to be organized upon considerations which are basically incompatible with the very principles that all agree are the foundation of the American democratic system. Sarason (1971), for example, found the following underlying assumptions in the typical classroom:
- the teacher always knows best
- children are not able to participate constructively in the development of the classroom rules
- children want and expect the teacher to determine the rules of the game
- children are not interested in how the classroom is run

- children should be governed by what a teacher thinks is right or wrong; a teacher should not be governed by what children think is right or wrong
- the ethics of adults are obviously different from and superior to the ethics of children
- children should not be given responsibility for something they cannot handle or for which they are not accountable.
- if classroom rules were handled differently, chaos might result

Such assumptions make it clear that although we may preach democracy, we are failing to practice it. It is wishful thinking to expect children to become responsible citizens if they are schooled in a non-democratic environment which stifles the skills and attitudes on which responsibility depends.

In order to move away from the all-too-common school described by Sarason toward the one described by Tyler requires a commitment on the part of the school community—the same kind of commitment given to the teaching of reading, writing, and arithmetic. Here, the principal can lead. To maximize the potential of the school as an agent for the development of the knowledge, skills, and attitudes of democratic citizens, schools must do more than teach academic knowledge and skills related to democracy. The total school, led by the principal, must demonstrate democratic values.

References

Combs, A. The human aspect of administration. *Educational Leadership,* 1970, *17,* 197–205.

Doll, R. *Leadership to improve schools.* Worthington, OH: Charles A. Jones, 1972, p. 283.

Ehman, L. Political education research and citizenship education. In Presseisen, B. (ed.). *School governance and classroom climate.* Philadelphia: Research for Better Schools, Inc., 1980, 111–112.

Fenton, E. The implications of Lawrence Kohlberg's research for civic education. In *Education for responsible citizenship.* New York: McGraw Hill, 1977.

Fenton, E. *The relationship of citizenship education to values education.* Philadelphia: Research for Better Schools, Inc., 1977, p. 6.

Fischer, L., and Fischer, B. Governance in elementary schools. In C. Anderson and L. Falkenstein (eds.). *Daring to Dream.* American Bar Association, Chicago, 1980.

Fox, R., et al. *School climate improvement: A challenge to the school administration.* Bloomington, IN: Phi Delta Kappa, 1974.

Goodlad, J. Can our schools get better? *Phi Delta Kappan,* 1979, *53,* 346.

Goodlad, J. *The dynamics of educational change.* New York: McGraw-Hill, 1974.

Grambs, J., Carr, J., and Fitch, R. *Modern Methods in Secondary Education.* New York: Holt, Rinehart and Winston, 1970.

Holman, E. L. The school ecosystem. In Foshay, A. (ed.). *Considered action for curriculum improvement.* Alexandria, VA: ASCD, 1980, 23–24.

Jackson, P. *Life in classrooms.* New York: Holt, Rinehart and Winston, 1968.

Kelley, E. *Improving school climate.* Reston, Va.: National Association of Secondary School Principals, 1980.

McGregor, D. *The human side of enterprise.* New York: McGraw-Hill, 1960.

Mosher, R. A democratic high school: Dam it, your feet are always in the water. In Mosher, R. (ed.). *Adolescents' development and education: A. Janus Krot,* Berkeley, CA: McCutchan, 1979.

National Education Association, Commission on the Reorganization of Seconday Education. *Cardinal principles of secondary education,* U.S. Bureau of Education, Bulletin 35, 1918, p. 14.

Neill, S. B. Violence and vandalism: Dimensions and correctives. *Phi Delta Kappan,* 1978, 302–303.

Riddick, J. Moral education will be the trend. *The Individualized Learning Letter,* 1979, *8* (March), 7.

Sarason, S. *The culture of the school and the problem of change.* Boston: Allyn and Bacon, 1971, p. 176.

Schmuck, R., and Schmuck, P. *A humanistic psychology of education: Making the school everybody's house.* Palo Alto, CA: National Press Books, 1974.

Shaheen, J. Cottage Lane: A student government program that works. *Social Education,* 1980, *44,* 387–390.

Sweeney, J. Research synthesis on effective school leadership. *Educational Leadership,* 1982, *39,* 346–352.

Tyler, R. The total educational environment. In Brown, B. F. (ed.). *Education for responsible citizenship.* New York: McGraw-Hill, 1977.

U.S. Senate, 94th Congress, 1st Session, Committee to Investigate Juvenile Delinquency, *Preliminary Report: Our Nation's Schools—A report card— "A" in school violence and vandalism.* Washington, DC: U.S. Government Printing Office, April, 1975.

Cooperative small group projects in which contributions from all stu-dents are needed can help improve affective relationships within a class.

CHAPTER SIX

It All Fits Together: A Case Study of Citizenship Experiences in Upper Valley High School[1]

Ellen Grundfest Sampson & Doug Jenisch

"Dear Mrs. McHenry:
We regret to inform you that your husband, Joseph, has been found disobeying the prohibition against eating or drinking in the halls at Upper Valley High   "

The Council of Upper Valley High School"

"We had a problem recently with litter in the halls. A lot of it was refuse left by people eating in the halls. I decided, with the Council's agreement, that eating in the halls would be prohibited. Food could be transported through the halls, but no actual eating or drinking could take place there. Letters would be sent home to the parents of people caught disobeying the new policy. Well, I thought it was a fine solution to the problem. Then one morning, shortly after the policy began, I stepped into the hall from my office carrying a cup of coffee. I took a drink, and got caught violating the new policy. They sent a letter home to my wife!"

Joe McHenry, Principal of Upper Valley High School, laughed as he finished telling his story. A friendly man with a confident, positive attitude toward his job, he clearly loved his work and was very proud of Upper Valley High. He encouraged visitors to check in with the main office and to visit with administrators, teachers, and students.

Upper Valley looks much like any other high school in a New England town. It has a brick front and is colonial in style. Part of it was built in the 19th century, and part of it was added in the 1950s. Outside, it looks rather attractive; inside, it is shabby and cluttered. Students and teachers dress casually; jeans are popular, but skirts and slacks are common, too. Some teachers are called by their first names.

---

[1]The name of the school and the names of its personnel have been changed for this case study.

As the school day begins, a visitor listens expectantly for the bell signaling the official start of the school day. The bell never rings. There are no bells, home rooms, or traditional class periods at Upper Valley High. There are neither study halls nor fixed lunch hours. The cafeteria has been replaced with a grill serving both fast foods and natural foods; all foods are labeled according to contents, calories, and nutritional value. The philosophy at Upper Valley High is that "adolescents can be trusted."

The Council Comes to Upper Valley High School

The Council is the central structure of student life at Upper Valley High. The goal of the Council system is to involve all elements of the school community in the decision-making process of the school. According to Principal McHenry, "We want everyone at Upper Valley to participate in making the policies that affect all of us. I don't want to sit here in the principal's office and say 'do this,' or 'don't do that.' Within the limits of state law and school board policy, teachers, students, and we administrators, too, have the power to influence how things are done at Upper Valley."

The Council was formed in 1971. It was in some ways the culmination of a period of change which began at Upper Valley in the late 1960s. A long-time teacher recalls that "until then, Upper Valley was a very traditional school. The principal made most of the decisions. Students had limited choice in academic matters and little power in school governance. They were assigned to various programs and to one of five ability-level groupings or tracks. It was very hard to move from one track to another, since grades were weighted according to degree of difficulty of the track."

In the late 1960s the educational upheaval that was occurring all over the country came to Upper Valley High. The School Board undertook an extensive study of the school. A new principal was hired and wide-ranging changes were made. The tracking system was eliminated. Dress codes, hall passes, study halls, home rooms, many required courses, and the traditional school day of five one-hour class periods were abolished.

Under the new system 40 percent of each day became unscheduled time for teachers and students. Many elective courses were introduced, reflecting students' demand and teachers' interests. The day was composed of twenty-minute modules, with classes meeting for two, three, or four modules on three, four, or five days per week. Open classrooms replaced the traditional teacher-centered ones. Students who had been previously separated by tracking mixed with one another.

A teacher commented that "so many changes in such a short period of time aroused strong emotions, pro and con, among students, teachers and members of the community. All of a sudden, the school became the focus of community debate. Letters to the editor of the local newspaper were common. School Board meetings were jammed. School Board elections were hotly contested. Budgets passed by margins of one percent or less of the vote. People who visited the school found students sitting in the halls, dressed in a wide variety of styles, reading, eating, talking, or even playing cards."

Even in a homogeneous community like Upper Valley, a change in educational direction at the high school stirred up controversy. Citizens with a shared goal of a school providing high quality education disagreed about how to achieve that goal. The positive value placed on participation helped to encourage people to have their say.

Differences of opinion, however vehement, did not shatter the community. Few parents withdrew their children from the school. Private academies did not spring up. The consensus which binds the community of Upper Valley held firm. Gradually, the new system, with some modifications, took root at Upper Valley High.

Throughout the controversy, the principal worked to build support and to nurture the new system at Upper Valley. After three years, the original innovators moved on to other jobs. A new principal and assistant principal came to Upper Valley. The new principal, Joseph McHenry, supported the changes at the high school.

McHenry recalled, "I did make some adjustments. There were some obvious problems with the system. Some students needed help in budgeting their unscheduled time. We needed new vocational education programs to help kids who weren't college-bound. We also needed to develop techniques to aid kids who were turned off by school. It is easy to forget those kids in a school like this, where many students go on to college."

A major concern of both McHenry and Larry Brown, the assistant principal, was to evolve some kind of student government at Upper Valley. In June 1970, the traditional student government which had existed for many years at Upper Valley voted to abolish itself. One member explained the decision. "We had no real power. Our elections were popularity contests." Brown suggested, "They felt that if they abolished the old student government, we [the administration] couldn't use them."

To give students some voice in school affairs, some faculty members proposed that student members be added to the Faculty Council, a group which advised the principal. One member from each grade was selected to serve on the Faculty Council. However, the new Student-Faculty Council lacked specific power, and student representation was severely limited. Gradually, a new system evolved from changes suggested by the principal and Council members.

Brown remembers that the first step was "to change the notion of being two groups—students and adults. We decided to make it a School Council."

The administration gave the Council the authority to "make decisions on all matters affecting student and faculty life not controlled by local or state education policy at Upper Valley High School." The principal could veto a decision made by the Council. The Council could, by a two-thirds vote, override that veto. The Council at Upper Valley High School became a true legislative body. At the request of the principal or the Council, a matter could be referred to the School Board for resolution—a kind of judicial process.

When the Council was initiated, it was linked to a caucus system. Brown explained that "all people in the school, students, teachers, administrators and staff, were randomly placed in caucuses of about 50 people. The caucuses elected representatives to the Council. They met weekly to discuss issues with their representatives, hear reports from the Council, and make suggestions about future action. The goal of the caucus system was to treat everyone in the school equally and give everyone a chance to participate."

The caucus system ran into trouble rather quickly, McHenry recalled. "It was complicated to manage. People didn't feel loyalty to the caucuses and attendance was poor." The caucus system was replaced by the current more traditional method of electing Council members.

Any member of the Upper Valley High community—students, staff, or faculty—may place his or her name in nomination for the Council. A school-wide election is held each spring. Those students who will be juniors or seniors the next fall each select four members from their own classes. Those who will be sophomores select three members. The faculty selects three members. In addition, all vote for seven at-large members. Freshmen elect three members in the fall. Brown stresses, "Members don't know whether they were elected by their obvious constituencies, such as a class or the faculty, or as an at-large member."

The Council hired an executive, paid with school funds, to help carry out its program. The members select a moderator, an assistant moderator, and a recorder. The Council has five committees. The committees deal with such concerns as student life, student activities, administration, housekeeping, and curriculum. As issues arise, they are referred to an appropriate committee. The committee studies the issue and reports back to the Council. Generally, the Council accepts committee recommendations.

The Council meets weekly. Brown said that "the schedule is arranged so that no Council members have classes at the time of the meeting." The Council's meetings in the auditorium conflict at times with play rehearsals or other activities. McHenry says, "When we renovate the building, the Council will have a more appropriate place to meet. This school is not yet physically suited for the kind of system we have here now."

The Council At Work

The Candy Machine: A Veto Overriden

The Council at Upper Valley voted to install a candy machine in the grill. The candy machine would serve two purposes. As one member put it, "We eat candy. If we put in the machine, we provide a service for the students. We also get some profit from the machine which we can use to improve student activities." After some debate over the nutritional benefits or lack thereof of candy, the machine won easily. Another student summed it up, "We know candy is bad for you, but it is our business, not the school's, to decide if we eat it."

After much thought, McHenry vetoed the Council's decision to install the candy machine. "I knew I would probably be overridden, but I was under pressure from people in the community. There are a lot of people concerned about nutrition in this town who claim the school should set a good example for the students by not making unhealthy foods readily available. So I vetoed the candy machine."

The Council found McHenry's arguments unconvincing. They voted easily to override his veto. "We don't want people outside our school to tell us what we should or shouldn't eat," said one member. After considerable discussion, a couple of changes were made in the original candy machine proposal. The Council decided to offer health snacks like granola bars and sunflower seeds in addition to candy in the machine. They also decided to label the contents of each item sold. With those adjustments, the principal's veto was overriden.

The principal made no further objection. The candy machine was installed in the grill. McHenry feels no anger at his inability to control the system. He participated in the decision-making process as an administrator sensitive to the opinions of the community. The students participated to protect their desire to have a candy machine. He laughingly remarked that, "they threw in the granola bar as a sop to the principal."

People of the community also accepted the installation of the candy machine. They did not choose to challenge the whole decision-making process at Upper Valley High over this issue. It is interesting to note that even on a relatively simple issue, the Council tried to respond to its critics, outside the school and within it, by including some non-candy items in the machine. Preserving the consensus is important, even if not consciously so, to the Council. The Council seemed aware that a participant system works best if compromises are sought.

The Soccer Team Imbroglio: The Principal Supported

The soccer team at Upper Valley won the state championship. Larry Brown, the assistant principal, described what happened next. "Suddenly bottles of champagne appeared. People were pouring it over each other, as well as taking swallows, and generally having a good time. There were rumors that the coach was seen handing a glass to a student. It was all in fun. The kids were just doing what they've watched professional teams do to celebrate a victory."

Upper Valley High, however, was not a pro team and laws had been broken. There were state laws against alcoholic beverages at public events, against high school students drinking, and against alcohol in public schools. An observer from the State High School Athletic Association watched the celebration and wrote a report. The executive director of the Association supported strict enforcement of the no-alcohol rule. Upper Valley High School received a letter asking it to "defend itself."

Brown remembered that "Joe McHenry and I thought the matter was serious, but we wanted to handle it on a local rather than a state level. Joe began an investigation. He asked for reports from the team captains, the coach, teachers, and parents who were there. We didn't get much. The parents who supplied the stuff did not come forward. The coach was exonerated, but it was clear we had to take some disciplinary action."

Joe McHenry, with the support of his assistant, Larry Brown, focused on two levels of the problem. First, he felt that the individual players who had been involved would have to be reprimanded in some way. Second—and more important from his perspective—the team as a whole would have to accept responsibility in the form of punitive action for the incident.

All the individuals on the team were placed on probation for the remainder of the year. Larry Brown explained, "Probation meant that if they were involved in one more troublesome incident, they would be unable to participate in any other school affairs for the rest of the year." The probation would not appear on their permanent records. This aspect of the principal's decision was relatively uncontroversial.

The second phase of the punishment dealt with team responsibility. As Joe McHenry remarked, "I am very concerned with group responsibility. I think our students today may not place enough importance on the need to be responsible to a group rather than just to one's self or one's immediate family. It was decided that the team as a whole would be prohibited from participating in any post-season play next year."

A storm broke around that decision. A cry of "unfair" arose at once from the students and from the community. The future players and their parents were especially irate. Of the championship team, only about five kids would be returning to play next fall. A common cry was that the principal's decision "penalized kids who weren't even involved."

The Council did not become involved in the incident until the controversy reached its height. At that point, Mr. Jones, a teacher serving as Council executive upon request of the Council, encouraged the Council to involve itself and to formulate a policy. A Council member remembers that "it took us too long to jump into the thing. Next time, we'll get in right away."

Once the Council did become involved, it played a significant role. It undertook its own investigation. The debate was long and passionate. At one meeting, the Council voted to express its disagreement with Joe McHenry's decision to punish next year's team. As Joe McHenry remembered it, "I walked by when one of the members was posting the decision and I said, 'You know, you could reconsider that vote one more time.' I lobbied those kids hard, trying to keep them with me. I needed them."

Another meeting was held. This time the Council voted to support the principal. The Council resolution was as follows:

> The Council of Upper Valley High supports Principal Joseph McHenry and the School Board in principle on their handling of the recent soccer-champagne incident. While we question the justice of punishing next year's soccer team, most of whose members are totally innocent in the matter, we also feel the Principal and School Board acted in the best possible manner under the circumstances.

The Council supported the principal once again several months later when they were asked to reexamine their decision. They reached the following conclusion:

> We feel that under the circumstances there was no other effective response Principal McHenry could have made to the incident. Unless the adults who supplied the champagne—the real culprits in the incident—wish to step forward and admit their guilt, there is no reason to reconsider.

McHenry and Brown both stressed the importance of the Council's support. The principal's decision created considerable outrage in the community. Some parents called upon the School Board to make an independent investigation. By declining to do so, the School Board placed itself, tacitly at least, on the principal's side in the debate. Brown speculated that "if the students had come out against the principal's decision, the School Board might have been less willing or able to support him." McHenry now says that if the Council had refused to support him, he would have rescinded his decision. "I don't think they perceived how much power they possessed," he remarked.

The imbroglio over the soccer team was much more serious than the decision to install a candy machine, involving a much larger segment of the community. In a more authoritarian system, the principal would have been able to issue his decision without encountering the controversy that echoed throughout Upper Valley. In a democratic system, however, dissent is acceptable and open.

There was dissent on the Council over McHenry's decision, but eventually the Council decided to support him. The ability of the school to unite itself helped to dilute community opposition to the decision. Groups, both within the school and outside of it, which sharply disagreed with McHenry's decision did not continue their organized opposition after the soccer affair ended. In a democratic environment, opposition groups tend to be fluid and short-lived. Once a crisis is over, consensus politics is reestablished. This pattern was seen in the soccer incident.

A Place to Smoke: An Unresolved Issue

At a recent meeting of the Council at Upper Valley, the major item on the agenda was the proposal to construct a smoking shelter. Smoking is a controversial issue at many high schools, and Upper Valley is no exception. Smoking is forbidden everywhere in the building, except in the teacher's room. Some teachers complain about not being able to smoke in their offices. Others complain about the smoke-filled teacher's room.

Students can smoke only in a small outdoor area behind the school. The smokers and others who congregate in that area are called "outbackers." The outbackers, as well as some non-smoking students who are sensitive to issues of student rights, feel that if teachers can have a place to smoke in the building, students should too. It goes against everything that Upper Valley stands for, they claim, to give teachers a smoking privilege denied to students.

At one time, the Council passed a motion requesting that an indoor smoking area be provided for students. McHenry vetoed the request. He explained that there was no space available in the school for a smoking area. The Council was convinced. It did not try to override the veto. Instead, they solicited alternate solutions. The outbackers suggested that a shelter be built outdoors to give smokers some protection at least from the New England weather. The outbackers raised some money. Preliminary designs were drawn up, but nothing happened.

During the winter, some outbackers approached a member of the Council once again about getting the Council to support construction of an outdoor smoking shelter. Several members of the Council, mostly non-smokers themselves, agreed to reopen the issue. As a leader of the pro-shelter group put it, "We represent the outbackers, too, and we should try to help them with their problems." Some members of the Council saw the smoking shelter issue as one which the Council could use to broaden its constituency in the school. As one member said, "It is a chance to show we care about and want to represent all the students—even those who don't participate much in school affairs."

The outbackers seemed less concerned about getting the administration to agree to a shelter than did the Council. One outbacker remarked, "It wouldn't work; it would just get all messy. What we need is a place to smoke indoors." Several others said they would like a place to smoke indoors or out. They didn't care enough, however, to participate in an effort organized by the Council to get it. "I'm graduating, and I won't be here next year anyway," was a frequent comment. School in general seemed less important to many outbackers than it did to Council members. They were fundamentally uninterested in the Council.

Even with mixed support from their constituency, the Council pushed ahead. The issue of the shelter was discussed at considerable length. The superintendent of schools attended. "I used to favor some kind of smoking area, but now I'm not sure," he said. "I think perhaps no one should be allowed to smoke at all, anywhere on school grounds. The school should take the lead in limiting smoking, which is an unhealthy thing."

His comments triggered a discussion reminiscent of the debate over the candy machine. Who should tell students what to do? Shouldn't they be treated as mature people capable of making their own choices about the dangers of smoking? One member said, "I think forcing teachers to stop smoking might be illegal. As long as teachers have a place to smoke, students should too."

Larry Brown added more controversy by saying that he couldn't support a smoking shelter at this time because plans were under way to renovate the entire school area. He proposed that they wait and see whether the renovation plans contained a place for smoking indoors and/or outdoors.

A Council member responded, "The renovation is still in the future, and the outbackers need the shelter now." Brown then suggested that the Council was not yet in a position to act. "You need more data on building permits, costs, fire laws, and insurance." The issue was referred to committee for more study.

Some members, who felt that Brown had once supported them, considered that on this issue he was backing off and looking for ways to delay the shelter. Brown himself acknowledged, "I'm afraid some of them had received the impression that I'd support the shelter."

McHenry viewed the smoking shelter in a more positive light. He said, "I think we'll have some kind of outdoor shelter next winter, renovation or not." He had not attended the Council meeting and his view was much more optimistic than that which prevailed at the end of the meeting. He was aware that the superintendent and Brown were uncertain. He said, however, that if the Council moved to request the shelter, some agreement would be worked out. He was sensitive to the Council's need to show its power before the skeptical "outbackers."

Council members expressed serious doubts about the outcome of the controversy over the smoking shelter. "I'm not sure at all that we'll get it," concluded the shelter's strongest supporter on the Council. They were more optimistic about their ability to get a smoking area included in the renovation plans. As one member remarked, "We have learned that we have to get involved early and keep track of everything. We are keeping track of the renovation plans."

The unresolved smoking shelter issue differed from the soccer affair or the candy machine decision. The Council had not yet faced community response to its move to build a smoking shelter.

In the meantime, the Council seemed determined to push for the shelter—not so much because the "outbackers" wanted it desperately, but because the Council wanted to prove to Upper Valley High, and perhaps to itself, that all the students do have a voice in their school. The outbackers were not a well organized pressure group; on the contrary, they were an amorphous, non-threatening group, which tended not to want to participate in school affairs. It may be a unique feature of the participant system at Upper Valley that the representative organization tries to help a group of students, whether or not it is well organized, when it expresses a need.

The Actors Review the Council

The Administration

Joe McHenry, the principal, helped to evolve the Council system and was deeply involved in nurturing it. "I'm trying now to get the School Board to make it a permanent part of the school so that it can survive a more hostile administration."

McHenry admitted readily that his small, academically oriented high school was not a typical high school. He disagreed, however, with the notion that a Council system can work only in conditions like those found at Upper Valley High. "What I see as crucial to the success of the system is not so much the kind of students, but the kind of administrator. If the administrator insists on keeping all power centralized, this kind of system won't work." Clearly, McHenry is comfortable about sharing power. He is willing to submit to vetoes and to lobby students. He sees participation by all groups within the school community as entirely positive.

McHenry viewed the Council in terms of his overall philosophy of education in high schools, which was based on the following assumptions: (1) Students, faculty and community should be full partners in decision-making.
(2) Professional expertise should be respected and sought out. Each human being should seek to use the resources of professionals and to be a resource for others.

(3) Role differences among people should be reordered and shuffled from time to time. All should experience the roles of teacher, learner, and citizen.

(4) A large number and variety of roles should be identified and formalized so as to provide status for many people at any given time. The division of labor should be such that tasks are meaningful, yet not an excessvie burden on any individual.

(5) The communication system should permit and encourage participation by all. Traditional limitations of democracy (e.g., constraints of size, time, and inefficiency) must be surmounted.

(6) A variety of ways to initiate change should exist and be widely publicized in the school.

(7) The governance model must be adequately supported—in terms of time, people, budget, space, sanction, etc.

(8) Finally, the governance model should facilitate the notion that the school is a center for inquiry—inquiry being the essential process for learning.

Brown pinpointed some problems the Council faces. He said, "It doesn't do a good job of selling itself. It hasn't developed a fast feedback system to its constituencies." One idea he has for improving the visibility of the Council is to get a closed-circuit television system to broadcast Council meetings. Brown saw himself as a founder, friend, and advocate of the Council. He was proud of the Council and enjoyed working with it. His style was different from McHenry's, but they worked together to make the system go.

Teachers

One young teacher remarked, "I feel lucky to teach in this school." Her sentiments were shared by many of her colleagues. The teachers appreciated the freedom to teach in a relatively unstructured environment. They enjoyed working with large numbers of bright, motivated students. Discipline was not a major problem, and the administration was cooperative.

A majority of the teachers supported the Council system. Several of them had served or were serving on it. Some had served as the paid executive to the Council. On many issues, coalitions of Council members cross student-faculty lines. On occasion, some teachers have found the Council's authority offensive or intrusive. If the Council is active in eliminating smoking from the teacher's room, it will surely antagonize teachers who smoke.

When a student complained to Mr. McHenry about the teachers and courses at Upper Valley, McHenry responded by telling him to do something about his complaints for a change. The student undertook an evaluation of teachers at Upper Valley. He brought his project to the Council, which decided to sponsor it. Most of the teachers found this acceptable, but a few were outraged, both by the Council supporting the project and by their correct perception that McHenry had at least triggered the action.

One teacher remarked, "There are still a few teachers here who prefer the old way, when the school was your traditional elitist institution. As they retire or leave, we are replacing them with people who like the system." McHenry and Brown praised the teachers as being "a competent, dedicated, cooperative group." Students, too, spoke highly of most of them; most of the evaluations were excellent.

Students

At Upper Valley, 85 percent of the 600 students go on to post-secondary education. Half of that group will attend competitive, prestigious colleges and universities. Brown explained, "There are three kinds of kids at Upper Valley. There are kids from upper-middle-class homes who do pretty well in school. They are active in sports and other school affairs. This group is quite large. Then there are kids from lower-middle-class homes who have some concern with education, but who are aware that 'they don't measure up.' They are a small group at Upper Valley. The third group is the 'outbackers.' The 'outbackers' come from a variety of backgrounds. They are alienated from most of their peers. They tend to cluster around the smoking area behind the school."

A teacher stressed that there were "all kinds of kids with all kinds of interests at Upper Valley—some who take courses at the college when they exhaust the high school's offerings in their specialties; others who seek out the remedial reading program because they read only at grade-level." Sixty percent of Upper Valley's students read at the twelfth-grade level in the ninth grade.

Upper Valley also has a program for students who are turned off by the school. As Brown explained it, "We don't let kids drop out. We give them a year's leave of absence. During the year, they keep in touch with one staff member or faculty member from the school. Most of them return to Upper Valley after one year. Our dropout rate is almost zero." Brown and McHenry also stressed that their school does provide programs for students who are not college-bound. Much of this type of training occurs at a vocational center in a nearby town. McHenry noted proudly, "We have well-equipped auto mechanics and machine shops. We are trying harder each year to help our students who need technical and agricultural training. We want them to be an important group at Upper Valley, too."

A survey of opinion at Upper Valley revealed that students felt quite well informed about the school. They perceived their Council as more involved with decision-making than are most student councils. They felt that the administration offers strong, but not paternalistic, leadership. The survey also suggested that there is a high level of participation in school affairs among students and teachers at Upper Valley and that participation and involvement in decision-making are increasing.

A majority of students felt that groups make more decisions than individuals, that influence is widely divided, and that majority rule is the standard for decision-making. They identified the following as important traits for a school leader to possess: a likeable personality, skill in working with people, an ability to follow through on projects, the capacity for good ideas and a willingness to share them, and dedication. Being smart, or earning good grades or coming from a well-known family was seen as less important, while having money was least important of all. Students perceived that at least half of the school population possessed leadership traits.

Many students at Upper Valley are proud of the Council. The moderator commented, "We are lucky to be going to school here." A member who has gone to other schools remarked, "This is the most unusual school I've ever been in." A majority of the students felt that communication within the school was adequate.

There were some students who had only a vague understanding of the Council and were not interested in learning more. Those who were interested and involved liked the system. They saw room for improvement, however. "We don't respond to student needs quickly enough, and we don't represent all the students." They also sensed how heavily the Council relied upon the commitment of the administration. The moderator summed it up: "Mr. McHenry and Mr. Brown are behind it all the way. I worry about what would happen if we got a principal who wanted to go back to the old days."

The Community

The two major towns in the school district are Upper Valley and Riverton. They are located across the river from each other and have been interrelated for 200 years. They were connected first by a rope-drawn ferry and later by a bridge. In spite of their closeness, the two towns have developed in quite different ways.

Upper Valley is a professionally oriented town. A college, a medical center comprising research, teaching, and treatment facilities, and a federally funded research laboratory are the leading employers in Upper Valley. Riverton was historically a farming community. After 1900, agriculture declined steadily. Children moved off the farms into rapidly developing mill and factory towns elsewhere in New England. While Upper Valley's population continued to grow, Riverton's decreased by almost 50% in less than 100 years. Gradually, the professional community in Upper Valley began to expand to Riverton.

The population of both communities is now composed largely of middle-

and upper-income families. Many of the teachers at Upper Valley High cannot afford to live in the district. There is considerable ethnic and social diversity in Upper Valley and Riverton. There is a small, but growing population of Oriental and black professionals; other residents come from all parts of the United States and from many foreign countries. At Upper Valley High the majority of the students are white; some of the black students who do attend come from urban ghettoes elsewhere and attend Upper Valley as part of a special program.

McHenry observed that "there is an intense concern about education in the Upper Valley school district. Not everyone, however, means the same thing by 'education.' Some prefer to stress the three 'R's.' Others admire the kind of education available at New England's famous private schools. Still others want a more experimental kind of education. There is a lot of pressure on the school to satisfy everyone."

Some Final Thoughts

Principal McHenry expressed hope that the future would see an ever stronger Council at Upper Valley. "I hope to get the Council institutionalized so that it is as much a part of Upper Valley as the principal's office. I look forward to seeing increasing numbers of students and faculty participate actively in the system. I would hope that more and more issues that affect all of us at Upper Valley would be resolved by the Council."

The students were worried about what would happen when a new principal and different teachers who didn't support the Council came to Upper Valley. Some students were uncertain as to how well the Council would work if a major issue like the controversy over the soccer team were to arise again. As one observer of the Council system remarked, "What if the Council refuses to support the principal on an issue where he feels that he cannot give in or compromise? Consequently, McHenry worked to make the Council independent of administrative support.

According to teachers, students, and administrators, the more democratic system at Upper Valley had benefits in addition to the level of participation that it provided at the school. Students learned to take on responsibility. The reading specialist said, "I graduated from Upper Valley before the changes. My younger brother graduated under the new system. They were much better able to use their time in college than I was. They worked out a lot of things in high school that most kids don't learn until they get to college. They learned to select courses, to work independently, and to manage and schedule time." A student who transferred to Upper Valley in the eleventh grade added, "When I first came here, it was confusing. No one said, 'Be here now,' 'do this,' 'don't do that.' At first I wasted a lot of time. Then I learned. I'm glad we moved to Upper Valley."

The council system . . . provides the students with a political education that may influence their behavior as adults.

The Council system at Upper Valley provided students with a political education that may influence their behavior as adults. One Council leader remarked, "I won't be active in student government in college unless the student government has real power, but I might get involved in community politics."

An observer at Upper Valley might wonder whether this more democratic system could work in other schools. Is the system at Upper Valley High School a product of the middle-class values of the people in the school community and the small size of the student body? Principal McHenry discounted this notion. He believed that a council system with appropriate responsibilities and powers, introduced gradually and with consistent commitment from the administration, can win the confidence of students, teachers and community nearly anywhere. McHenry was convinced that school administrators who share his philosophy that "adolescents can be trusted" could implement a council system in any type high school.

A final note can be added. In fact, before McHenry left Upper Valley High School, the School Board did indeed institutionalize the governance system represented by the Council, which then became board policy. As a result, an administration acting alone at the high school cannot dismantle it. The Council still operates at Upper Valley.

CHAPTER SEVEN

Resources for Teachers and Administrators

I. Books

Bebermeyer, R. *Leadership For School Climate Improvement.* St. Louis: CEMREL, Inc., 1982.

Offers a review of literature under three headings—leadership, school climate, and improvement. Includes a description of school climate improvement efforts in Akron, Cincinnati, Detroit, and Kansas City, MO. Bibliography.

Bloom, B.S. *Human Characteristics and School Learning.* New York: McGraw-Hill, 1976.

Examines reasons why students are failing in our educational system and why students are being socially promoted. Bloom maintains his faith in our educational system, offering suggestions on how school might help those students who have been socially promoted. Though Bloom addresses educational theorists and researchers, he also offers many practical suggestions for teachers.

Brown, B.F., ed. *Education for Responsible Citizenship.* New York: McGraw-Hill, 1977.

Major theme of this book is that today's students are totally unprepared for citizenship. While there are many reasons for the lack of citizenship understanding, Brown claims that part of the problem is centered on the poor quality of traditional citizenship education. Articles explore possibilities for improvement, including federally-funded national civics programs.

Brubaker, D. L., and Nelson, R. H. *Creative Survival in Educational Bureaucracies.* Berkeley, CA: McCutchan, 1974.

Brubaker and Nelson offer educators a down-to-earth, common sense approach for surviving the problems and difficulties within the educational bureaucracy, while maintaining a professional attitude. Book is ideal for teachers and administrators of all school levels. It contains case studies, inventories, and discussion of various educational problems.

Butts, R. F. *The Revival of Civic Learning.* Bloomington, IN: Phi Delta Kappa, 1980.

The author pleads that citizenship continue to be taught in the schools. Book contains a history of the idea of citizenship and reviews citizenship education in the United States. It also contains suggestions for promoting citizenship and responsibility.

Clark, F. J. *Improving School Climate.* (Operations Notebook No. 19), Association of California School Administrators, October, 1977.

A training module which presents a variety of techniques by which administrators can assess and improve school climate.

Committee on Citizenship Education of the Council of Chief State School Officers. *Effective Citizenship Education: A Basic Goal of Education in the United States.* Washington, DC: Council of Chief State School Officers, 1976.

Lists seven goals of citizenship education and a series of suggestions for its improvement. A national conference on citizenship education followed this position statement.

Constans, H. P. *Fit for Freedom.* Washington, DC: University Press of America, 1980.

Asks public schools to produce students who are capable of functioning as responsible, democratic citizens. Constans examines how well public educators are succeeding in this task and proposes changes to enable a system to produce more responsible citizens. Book is intended for teachers as well as those preparing to become teachers.

Dreeben, R. *On What is Learned in School.* Reading, MA: Addison-Wesley, 1968.

An analysis of the ways in which the schooling process influences the learning of norms related to democratic political life. Focuses on the contribution of school life to the normative psychological capacities which enable people to participate in public institutions.

Entwistle, H. *Political Education in a Democracy.* London: Routledge & Kegan Paul, 1971.

Author presents a theoretical and practical case for democratic participatory experiences in schools. Although written about Great Britain, the book's review of the limitations of traditional political education and suggestions for more student governance are appropriate for the U.S.

Epstein, Joyce L., and McPartland, James. *Quality of School Life.* Baltimore: The Johns Hopkins University Center for Social Organization of Schools, 1976.

Contains a 27-item survey instrument that measures student satisfaction, commitment to classwork, and relations with teachers. It can be used with students in grades 4–12.

Erickson, D. A., and Reller, T., eds. *The Principal in Metropolitan Schools.* Berkeley, CA: McCutchan, 1979.

A collection of readings designed not only for the principal in a metropolitan area but for those in many educational settings. Explores student rights, the economics of urban education, leadership, the expectations of teachers, and community relations.

Fox, R. S. et al. *School Climate Improvement: A Challenge to the School Administrator.* Bloomington, IN: Phi Delta Kappa, 1974.

Describes ways to provide significant improvements and leadership within the school climate. Principals, administrators and other educators who are concerned with improving school climate will find many practical suggestions and checklists.

Glasser, W. *Schools Without Failure.* New York: Harper & Row, 1969.

Largely based on examples and case studies, Glasser explores the premise that schools must support the idea of success rather than failure for their students. There are philosophical and practical suggestions for teachers and administrators for supporting success by their students.

Halpin, A. W., and Croft, D. B. *The Organization Climate of Schools.* Chicago: Midwest Administration Center of the University of Chicago, 1963.

A descriptive study of school climates based on survey data collected from teachers and administrators of 71 schools. Analysis of the data revealed six different types of school climates ranging from open to closed.

Jackson, P. *Life in Classrooms.* New York: Holt, Rinehart & Winston, 1968.

The classic study of the hidden curriculum. Jackson focuses on what students learn as a result of attempting to cope with power, crowds, and praise in the school environment.

Kelly, E. A. *Improving School Climate: Leadership Techniques for Principals.* Reston, VA: National Association of Secondary School Principals, 1980.

Publication is a thorough, though brief, description of the various dimensions of school climate. Includes practical suggestions for school administrators interested in promoting a positive learning environment. Offers a 22-step model for planning climate assessment or development projects. Bibliography.

Kohler, M., ed. *New Roles for Youth in School and Community.* New York: National Commission on Resources for Youth.

A collection of case studies about students involved in innovative projects in their communities.

Lezotte, L. W. et al. *School Learning Climate and Student Achievement.* Tallahassee, FL: SSTA Center, Teacher Education Project, Florida State University, 1980.

A comprehensive look at school learning climate and its impact on student achievement. Includes a review of the literature and a consideration of the problems that accompany organizational change. Annotated bibliography.

Massialas, B. G., ed. *Political Youth, Traditional Schools.* Englewood Cliffs, NJ: Prentice-Hall, 1972.

A collection of political socialization research articles dealing with formal and informal effects of schools on political knowledge and attitudes of students.

Mosher, R. L., ed. *Moral Education: A First Generation of Research and Development.* New York: Praeger, 1980.

A collection of articles dealing with the application of Kohlberg's ideas of just community and moral education in American schools. Contains theoretical discussions, reflections on school experiences, viewpoints, and research reports.

Newmann, F., and Oliver, D. *Clarifying Public Controversy.* Boston: Little, Brown, & Co., 1970.

Book offers both theory and application for the teaching of controversial issues in the classroom.

Newmann, F. *Education for Citizen Action: Challenge for Secondary Curriculum,* Berkeley, CA: McCutchan, 1975.

An argument for comprehensive instruction in citizenship education. Latter is broadly defined as having community outreach and community experiences for students. Teachers will find a practical list of student projects including community work, field research, and other methods of active learning.

Overly, N. V., ed. *The Unstudied Curriculum: Its impact on Children.* Washington, DC: Association for Supervision and Curriculum Development, 1980.

Articles focus on the effect of the hidden curriculum on student learning, growth, and behavior. Authors include Philip Jackson, Edgar Z. Friedenberg, Barbara Biber, Patricia Minuchin, Robert Rosenthal, Robert Dreeben, and Lawrence Kohlberg.

Pressiesen, B. Z., ed. *School Governance and Classroom Climate.* Philadelphia: Research for Better Schools, Inc., 1980.

Articles address two basic questions: How does the way in which a school operates influence the development of basic democratic beliefs? How do the structure and management of the classroom influence the climate of the school and citizenship education?

Purkey, William W. *Self-Concept and School Achievement.* Englewood Cliffs, NJ: Prentice-Hall, 1970.

Examines the impact of the student's assessment of self on academic success. Explains the ways in which self-concept develops and the role of the school in shaping self-concept. Includes practical, research-based suggestions to reinforce positive and realistic self-concepts in students.

Rutter, M. et al. *Fifteen Thousand Hours: Secondary Schools and Their Effects on Children.* Cambridge, MA: Open Books, 1979.

A report on research conducted in 12 London schools. Rutter believes that school processes influence a student's behavior and academic achievement more strongly than home environment. This is an important book for educators.

Sarason, S. B. *The Culture of the School and the Problem of Change.* Boston: Allyn & Bacon, 1971.

Considers the need for and process of reform in American schools. Sarason describes the difficulties that teachers, administrators, and other professional educators face when they try to balance their ideal expectations against the realities of school life. A readable book which offers practical advice and guidance to all professional educators.

Schmuck, R. A., and Schmuck, P. A. *Group Processes in the Classrooms.* Third Edition, Dubuque, IA: William C. Brown, 1979.

Describes group interaction in classrooms which facilitate and hinder cognitive and affective learning. Practical techniques are presented for utilizing or modifying those processes to increase effectiveness of teaching and learning.

Shaver, J. P., and Larkins, A. G. *Decision-Making in a Democracy.* Boston: Houghton Mifflin, 1973.

Presents a way of analyzing enduring public issues in a reading and discussion format. Specific instructional materials and teacher guidelines are included.

Slavin, R. *Using Student Team Learning.* Baltimore: Johns Hopkins University Center for Social Organization Schools, 1980.

Describes procedures for implementing three team learning strategies: Teams-Games-Tournament; Student Teams-Achievement Divisions; and Jigsaw. A teacher needs only this booklet in order to utilize any of the strategies. Available for $2.00 from the Center for Social Organization of Schools, Johns Hopkins University, 3505 North Charles Street, Baltimore, MD, 21218.

Torney, J. V., Oppenheim, A., and Farnen, R. *Civic Education in Ten Countries.* New York: John Wiley & Sons, 1975.

A cross-national research study of the civic education of students in ten countries including the U.S. Data from over 30,000 responses is the basis for comparative analysis of knowledge and attitude outcomes.

II. Articles

Allman-Snyder, A. et al. "Classroom structure and children's perceptions of authority: An open and closed case." *Urban Education,* 1975, *10,* 131–149.

Bean, J. A., Lipka, R. P., and Ludewig, J. W. "Synthesis of research of self-concept." *Educational Leadership,* 1980, *38,* 84–89.

Broudy, H. "Educating for responsibility." *Responsibility Education Newsletter,* 1976, *1,* 747–757.

Caramia, J. A., Jr., and Knight, C. "Group processes in teaching social studies: An instructional unit." *Georgia Social Science Journal,* 1980, *17,* 1–5.

Cawelti, G. "Training for effective school administrators." *Educational Leadership,* 1982, *39,* 324–329.

Ehman, L. H. "The American school in the political socialization process." *Review of Educational Research,* 1980, *50,* 99–119.

Gillespie, J. A., and Mehlinger, H. "Teach about politics in the real world— the school." *Social Education.* October, 1972, 598–604.

Giroux, H., and Penna, A. "Social education in the classroom: The dynamics of the hidden curriculum." *Theory and Research in Social Education,* 1979, 7 (1), 21–42.

Hawley, W. D. "Political education and school organization." *Theory into Practice,* 1971, *10,* 328–335.

Hepburn, M, and Napier, J. "Patterns of student attitudes toward political institutions and participation." *Teaching Political Science,* 1982–83, *10,* 77–88.

Kohlberg, L., and Blatt, M. "The effects of classroom moral discussions upon children's level of moral judgment." *Journal of Moral Education,* 1975, *4,* 129–161.

Maynard, W. "The impact of humanistic school climate." *NASSP Bulletin,* 1976, *60* (April) 16–20.

Reimer, J. "Moral education: The just community approach." *Phi Delta Kappan,* 1981, *62,* 485–487.

Sergiovanni, T. J. "Ten principles of quality leadership." *Educational Leadership* 1982, *39,* 330–336.

Shaheen, J. "Cottage Lane: A student government program that works." *Social Education,* 1980, *44,* 387–390.

Shoemaker, J., and Fraser, H. W. "What principals can do: Some implications from studies of effective schooling." *Phi Delta Kappan,* 1981, *63,* 178–182.

Slavin, R. "Cooperative learning." *Review of Educational Research,* 1980, *50,* 315–342.

Sweeney, J. "Research synthesis on effective school leadership. *Educational Leadership."* 1982, *39,* 346–352.

Torncy, J. V. "The definition of citizen capacities and related psychological research in 'Behavior Variables Related to Citizen Education: Colloquium Papers.' " Philadelphia: Research for Better Schools, Inc., 1978.

Weissburg, R. "Adolescent experiences with political authorities." *Journal of Politics,* 1972, *34,* 797–824.

Wasserman, E. "Implementing Kohlberg's 'just community concept' in an alternative high school." *Social Education,* 1976, *40,* 203–207.

Yarrow, M.; Scott, P., and Waxler, C. "Learning consideration for others." *Developmental Psychology,* 1973, *8,* 240–260.

III. Special Issues of Periodicals

Journal of Research and Development in Education, issue on Social Interdependence in the Classroom, volume 12, no. 1, Fall, 1978.

LRE Report (Newsletter of the American Bar Association) issue on Law and the Democratic Classroom, Spring, 1981.

Moral Education Forum, issue on Creating a Just Community, 6 (4) Winter 1981–82.

Practical Applications of Research (Newsletter of Phi Delta Kappa) issue on Discipline, September, 1981.

Theory Into Practice, issue on Democracy in Education, volume 15, no. 1 February 1976.

IV. Materials for Classroom Instruction

A. *Print Materials*
LaRaus, R., and Remy, R. *Citizenship Decision Making.* Reading, MA: Addison-Wesley, 1978. (Teaching activities for middle grades).

National Association of Student Councils, 1904 Association Drive, Reston, VA.: *The Student Advocate* (student newsletter).

Brandwein, P., et al., *Individuals As Policy Makers.* New York: Harcourt Brace Jovanovich, 1977. (seventh grade volume of *Sources of Identity*.)

Improving Citizenship Education Project Elementary Teachers Handbook. 786 Cleveland Avenue, SW Atlanta, GA 30315: Fulton County School System, 1981, (book of lesson plans and teaching activities).

B. *Audio-Visual Materials*
Why We Have Laws: Shiver, Gobble, and Snore (filmstrip-audio cassette, elementary grades) Learning Corporation of America.

The Great Rights (film, secondary grades) Macmillan Films.

Vandalism, Stealing, Lying, and Hurting People (filmstrip-audio cassette, elementary grades) Learning Corporation of America.

Values in a Democracy (filmstrip-audio cassette, fits middle school and secondary level).
"Job-related Issues: What's Right"
"Personal Issues: What's Right?"
"National Issues: What's Right?"
"Local Issues: What's Right?"
"Legal Issues: What's Right"
—from Guidance Associates

Juvenile Problems and Law (filmstrip kit) Mineola, NY: West Publishing Company.

Youth Attitudes and Police (filmstrip kit) Mineola, NY: West Publishing Company.

The Law and Youth (filmstrip series, secondary grades) Chatsworth, CA: Opportunities for Learning, Inc., 1982.

Being Responsible (filmstrips-audio cassettes, elementary grades) Boulder, CO: Learning Tree Filmstrips, 1979.

Foundations of Justice (filmstrip kit, middle school grades) Columbus, OH: Merrill Social Studies Catalog, Merrill Publishing Company, 1978.

In Search of Justice (filmstrip kit, secondary grades), Columbus, OH: Merrill Social Studies Catalog, Merrill Publishing Company, 1978.

Understanding the Law (filmstrip kit, elementary grades) Boulder, CO: Learning Tree Corporation, 1979.

Changing the Law (film, secondary grades), Santa Monica, CA: Bailey Film Associates.

The Political Animal (film, secondary grades) Middletown, CT: Xerox Films.

Voting at 18 (film, secondary grades) Chicago: Coronet Instructional Media.

Understanding Law (filmstrip kit, secondary grades) Chatsworth, CA: Opportunities for Learning, Inc., 1982.

Audio-Visual Producers

Bailey Film Associates
2211 Michigan Avenue
Santa Monica, CA 90406

Charles E. Merrill Publishing Company
1300 Alum Creek Drive
Columbus, OH 43216

Coronet Instructional Media
65 East South Water Street
Chicago, IL 60601
(Does Not Rent Films)

Guidance Associates
P.O. Box 300
White Plains, NY 10602

Learning Corporation of America
1350 Avenue of the Americas
New York, NY 10019

Learning Tree Filmstrips
934 Pearl Street
Box 1590
Dept. 500
Boulder, CO 80306

Macmillan Films, Inc.
34 MacQuesten Parkway South
Mt. Vernon, NY 10550

Opportunities for Learning, Inc.
8950 Lurline Avenue, Dept. K
Chatsworth, CA 91311
(213) 341-2535

West Publishing Company
170 Old Country Road
Mineola, NY 11501
(516) 248-1900

Xerox Films
Xerox Education Publications
245 Long Hill Road
Middletown, CT 06457

Epilogue

This Bulletin addresses a topic which has been of concern to social studies educators for many years. The ideal of educating the young for democratic citizenship by providing experiences in democratic participation is certainly not new. Over 60 years ago John Dewey, viewing schools as the important and difficult bridge between the family and democratic society, explained the need to attend to the informal education which takes place in schools as carefully as formal instruction or curriculum.

"There is a standing danger that the material of formal instruction will be merely the subject matter of the schools, isolated from the subject matter of life experience," Dewey warned in *Democracy and Education*. He stressed the importance of the learning environment in the development of dispositions necessary to a healthy democratic society, and it was a participatory environment which he considered truly "educative."

The purpose of the NCSS position statement and this volume is to reiterate and renew the commitment of our profession to schooling which is consistent with democratic principles. The volume was designed to offer ideas and practical information which can lead to better teaching of the skills and attitudes required of democratic citizens. Specifically, the ad hoc Committee on Democratization of Schools was charged with promoting an examination of the ways in which the environment of the whole school and individual classrooms contribute to or hinder democratic education. Our charge necessitated that we focus on the past, especially the recent past, looking for practices and ideas that could guide changes in the present, which, in turn, could improve outcomes in the future.

Enormity of Changes

Now in 1983 reflecting on the position statement written in 1978 and the completed chapters prepared in the three years that followed, I am struck by the enormity of the changes which have been taking place since this project was begun. This book was prepared within the context of a traditional perspective on leadership roles in schools. Schooling has been viewed as a process in which teachers channel information and ideas to students, guide them in developing skills to help gather more information, and attempt to motivate them to use the information to think and live more effectively. In this view the teacher has a pivotal role in the classroom as an authority or leader down the path of knowledge and critical thinking. As the teacher is group leader in the classroom, the principal is group leader in the school. In this context these leaders are considered to be in control of major social-political environmental factors. We consider that they can have a major impact on the *setting* for educational activities as well as the activities.

Today, in February 1983, I suspect that the context of education in schools is changing, and with it the leadership or authority positions of teachers and administrators are changing. In the years since this project was launched, a rapid and widespread change in techniques of obtaining, retaining, and communicating information has been taking place, and it is building the potential for remarkable change in our schools.

Role of Technology

Some educators suggest that computer technology and satellite tele-communications are just the latest in a long line of innovations—such as the overhead projector—which have neither changed teaching nor the context of education. It seems to me that the changes now taking place are vast societal changes in information processing which are being imposed on the schools. Teaching and learning procedures, in social studies and every school subject, are likely to change considerably within this decade.

What bearing does this have on the social-political environment of American schools and the whole question of making schooling more democratic? In the changing context of schooling new questions arise in regard to education for democratic citizenship. Will the electronic access to information, open to every young person who knows how to operate the computer keyboard, break down the age-old classroom authority structure in the classroom and even in the school, thus democratizing education? It seems likely that students will become more independent of teachers as a result of modified educational procedures for obtaining, storing, and utilizing knowledge. It also seems likely that the psychological distance between teachers and students will increase. In a similar manner, the distance between administrators and teachers will be increased as more of school management is handled electronically. How will such changes affect student attitudes, teacher attitudes, and administrator attitudes toward each other and toward participation in school?

New Inequities Ahead?

Will interaction with people from all over the world via satellite video telecommunication enrich and broaden experiences and perspectives of students thus strengthening their democratic attitudes and skills? Or, will the economically and socially advantaged students who have computers in their homes develop an edge on knowledge thus creating new types of inequities with which educators must deal?

Will greater technological communication enrich and improve the quality of knowledge access while dehumanizing the participants? Some suggest that with advanced widespread high technology education may become a small group process conducted in neighborhoods or in individual homes. How then can the skills and attitudes of democratic participation be taught?

The changes that are taking place around us are shaping a different context for American schooling in general and for social studies education in particular. It is important that we think about and utilize the case studies, research information, and personal perspectives of this book to think not only of educational improvement in the present but to prepare for education in the future.

American educators have no monopoly on the concern over democratic schooling. Educators of other democratic nations have similar interests in school and classroom practices which can better educate young people for democratic citizenship. An exchange of conceptual approaches and practical observations could enrich the understanding and efforts of social studies educators in all democratic countries. Such an exchange is an important additional consideration for the near future.

In summary, for those of us who worked on this project and for NCSS members in general, this Bulletin must not be thought of as the product of a completed project, it must serve as the beginning of reflections on directions for democratic schooling in the future.

Mary A. Hepburn

Editor, and Chair Ad Hoc Committee on Democratization of Schools
February, 1983

Index

Indexed by Leila Cabib. Design by E. S. Qualls set in 10 point ITC Garamond and printed by Carter Printing Company.